5 STRATEGIES FOR

STAYING EMPLOYED

IN TODAY'S ECONOMY

Nina
Price

ISBN - 10: 061531161X

ISBN - 13: 9780615311616

Limits of Liability/Disclaimer of Warranty

Author's Note

The anecdotes presented in this work are based on true events. However, the names of the people and/or places have been changed to protect those involved.

I get by with a little help from my friends.

~ The Beatles

Many of my friends, colleagues, and clients contributed to this book. Some shared their stories, others read and critiqued the manuscript, and others offered reality checks as needed. Huge thank yous and lots of hugs to all who assisted with this endeavor including but not limited to:

- Donna Kozik, Adam Urbanski. offered big challenges and inspiration.

- Krys Corbett, , Barbara Elsea, Howard Finck, Mike Kimball, Donna Montgomery, Gillian Muessig, and Mark Turner, offered insights.

- Kathy Abelson, Bob Dahlgren, Meg Karakekes, Terri Mullen, Evelyn Roberts, and Phyllis Thé gave me feedback.

- Tom Boures, Susan Daffron, Erin Ferree, Andrea Glass, Julie Hawkins, Vrinda Normand, Jacki Opferman, Francie Soito all have talents I admire and value, but don't possess.

I also offer huge thank yous and lots of hugs to those who wished not to be acknowledged by name.

Special thanks to my dear husband Rod Price who quietly supports my big ideas and patiently enjoys the journey.

Thank you all for your support during this whirlwind book creation process!

Contents

Chapter | 1

The Major Workforce Crisis That No One's Noticing

This book is for *professionals over 40* who have found that lately it's more difficult to get rehired or stay employed than it used to be, when they were younger.

It's for people who are *between jobs and feeling precarious*. They've worked diligently for two decades building solid careers, achieving their goals, and making their bosses look good only to be thanked with a "pink slip" as their employer routinely "cleaned house."

It's for people over 40 who are *underemployed and stuck*. They just want to be able to pay their bills and have health insurance. They stay in jobs where the work is boring beyond belief, they have co-workers they don't enjoy, and their commute is horrible. Many days they find that it's hard to look forward to going to work in the morning. People in this group may also have "golden handcuffs," a pension or payout of some sort that they are looking forward to at retirement, which they can't receive unless they stay in this job.

It's also for people who are still *hanging on to their jobs by their fingernails*. Regardless of whether or not they love their job, these people live in fear of the next layoff. It's not that their performance is an issue; these days managers may have "all star teams" and still be required to cut a percentage of their team at layoff time. Hence the constant fear of losing their job.

"The Age Discrimination in Employment Act of 1967 (ADEA) protects individuals who are 40 years of age or older from employment discrimination based on age. The ADEA's protections apply to both employees and job applicants. Under the ADEA, it is unlawful to discriminate against a person because of his/her age with respect to any term, condition, or privilege of employment, including hiring, firing, promotion, layoff, compensation, benefits, job assignments, and training." [1]

The ADEA notwithstanding, ageism is rampant in today's corporate layoffs and hiring. I think it needs to stop!

This book is also a *plea to corporate leaders*. Stop targeting older professionals in layoffs just because they cost too much. Frankly, you're killing the goose that lays your golden eggs! There are more effective ways to manage workforce attrition and retirement than through layoffs.

Baby boomers want to work longer and retire when they choose to. There are also over 76 million of them in the U.S. [2] Many are healthy and capable of contributing great work to your organization. Why not be creative and think of more effective ways to manage the later years of their careers so you get the best of their expertise? Why subject your experienced workers to the gruesome, confidence-deflating experience of collecting an unemployment check at a time in their lives when they often have the most financial responsibility?

With the graying of the workforce, experts are anticipating worker shortages within the next 10 years. Why not be proactive and develop ways of allowing the baby boomers to transition into a working retirement, which is what the research says they want to do? Why not smooth out the anticipated trends by using talented workers currently in your employ to do projects, training, and mentoring that's badly needed? You could even develop strategies which allow older workers to gradually transition from full time to part time, or to contract work. This would help to prevent worker shortages and allow you to get useful work done. Such strategies not only recognize the contribution of experienced workers, but allow them the dignity to retire when and how they choose to.

Why not constructively discourage complacency and encourage older workers to take responsibility for their careers by re-evaluating how they can best serve your company as they gradually transition into a working retirement?

With respect to rehiring older workers who are between jobs or who want to change jobs, I would like to see more companies be willing to hire experienced older workers into both full time and contract jobs.

Quit being so cheap! Like most short term thinking, it's not really serving you in the long run.

Chapter

| 2

Why You Need to Read This Book

Whether you're in need of a new job, trying to get back into the job market, secure where you are, or hanging on to your job by your fingernails—this book is for you. *This book is about proactively re-evaluating where you are, what no longer serves you, and what needs to change in your life so you can take better care of yourself and your career.*

Let's begin by getting to know three talented people who are facing classic issues that professionals are grappling with in today's economy. Which one is most like you?

Between Jobs and Feeling Precarious

I received a LinkedIn invitation from a former colleague the other day, whom I hadn't heard from in eight years. It was great to hear from William (who still doesn't like to be called Bill). I gladly accepted William's LinkedIn invitation and sent him an email telling him how I appreciated hearing from him. In the email, I asked what he was up to. In his return email, he asked if we could chat by phone after his kids' soccer practice.

When we talked, I wasn't surprised by his story. I've heard the "layoff story" from many talented professionals. William had been hit by a layoff a couple of months ago and was recovering. He'd never been through a layoff before. He'd never collected unemployment before. He admitted to me that collecting unemployment wasn't doing much for his self-esteem.

William is a really talented guy, and I reminded him of that fact. He's a great sales person and has very strong technical skills. He was working as a software development manager most recently, and being remote from the rest of the company made him an easy layoff target.

We talked about options. William has great sales skills and could easily get some technical consulting gigs to tide him through until he finds another full time job. I pointed out to him that he may discover he really prefers the flexibility of self-employment at this point in his career, while he figures out what he *really* wants to do next. I encouraged William to look at this "career reset" as an opportunity to do some re-evaluation about who he wants to become in the next phase of his career.

Like most people in their 40s and 50s, even though they know there's no such thing as "lifetime employment," William thought he had a steady gig with a prestigious multinational corporation. He'd probably become complacent. In hindsight, he now thinks he should have moved on to another company some years ago, to pursue some new challenges. Instead, he stayed put because where he was seemed to be working. So in effect, the company "pushed the career reset button on his career" for him.

If you're complacent and know you need to push the reset button on your career, but you're not doing it, or if like William, the reset button has been pushed for you, keep reading—you need what's in this book.

Underemployed with Golden Handcuffs

Maryanne is an attractive woman in her 60s, who always seemed a bit sad. She has many friends and takes several vacations a year because she likes to travel. She has a range of interests including decorating, gardening, hiking, and going to the theatre. She spends her free time pursuing these interests with her friends. I always wondered why I sensed a sadness about her. One day she came to see me at her wits end, and I found out what was bothering her.

I knew that recently, another company had acquired the company she'd worked for, for 20 years. The management of her company insisted that their employees not be let go, and be allowed to work until they retired with the generous health and retirement benefit plan of their original employer. Although the new company could reassign these employees to new jobs and locations, the employees got to keep their legacy benefits.

Maryanne was not too far from retirement. As a single woman, she was counting on the generous retirement benefits. The company that acquired her firm reassigned Maryanne to a new job in a new location much further from where she lived. In fact, her new commute was much worse than before, and there were no public transportation options. The new commute was along a route that is well known for heavy rush hour traffic. The new work location also didn't have good shopping or nice restaurants nearby as her previous location had.

Maryanne had told me she found her new job "not very interesting or challenging." In fact, she described it as "quite menial and boring," but she hastened to add, "I have a job, and I have great health and retirement benefits. How many people can say that?" But that day, Maryanne was at her wits end. Between her commute, the traffic, and her job, it had been a long day and she'd had enough. I sensed there was more and asked what else was bugging her. "I hate to say this," Maryanne grimaced, "and I've never admitted this before, but I can't stand my new co-workers! They're lazy, mean, backbiting, and complaining. I can't believe this, but today someone actually stole my lunch out of the fridge in the break room! I didn't get a nourishing lunch, which is probably why I'm crabby, but I can't believe anyone would do something like that at work!"

Maryanne has a job with "golden handcuffs." Many older workers find themselves in situations with "golden handcuffs." They don't want to walk away from benefits they now enjoy, or from their pension or other kinds of retirement payouts for which they've worked many years. Yet often, the day-to-day routine of their jobs feels unbearable to them.

They're marking time to collect a regular paycheck and get the benefits they want.

I asked Maryanne about the soonest date she could retire. "Three years from my next birthday, in 38 months," was her reply. "Is there any way you could leave sooner with full benefits?" I asked. Maryanne was doubtful but agreed to do some research. "Could you be reassigned to a location closer to your home?" I asked. "I doubt it," said Maryanne, "it looks like they'll be closing down the site where I used to work." "Are there any other jobs you could ask to do at the new company?" I asked. "I don't know, but I'll make some inquiries," she said.

If like Maryanne you're underemployed, with (or without) "golden handcuffs," if you're ready to re-evaluate and "push the reset button" on whatever's not working for you, keep reading.

Hanging on by Her Fingernails

Laura has a challenging professional job at a big name company. She's attractive, blonde, in great shape, has a solid résumé, and doesn't look like she's in her late 50s. She's a high level individual contributor who always seems to work for a management team who are younger than she is.

Her job skills are excellent for her high visibility role, however, she feels that her career has stalled. Additionally, everything she does is on a short deadline, and there are constantly multiple simultaneous deadlines. In recent years, she's had more trouble with insomnia. In fact, she's noticed that every time an upcoming layoff has been announced, she would start to feel anxious, her sleep would become unpredictable, and as a result, she was worried about her performance at work. Friends her age had been hit by the last five layoffs at her company. Even though her manager is pleased with her performance, the business she is working in has not been profitable during the last few quarters. She knows that management will have to lay off 10% of the group.

When she came to see me, she looked tired and worn out. Her eyes were lusterless, and her spirits were low. I asked her whether she had a "Plan B" in mind in the event she was hit by the next layoff. "Honestly, I've been too busy making my deadlines to even think about a Plan B," she said. I pointed out that she was taking care of her physical self by coming to see me, so perhaps she would take a moment or two to take care of her career by pondering a possible Plan B. She took a deep breath and thought for a few minutes, her eyes filled with tears. "No matter how hard I work or how great my results are, I still feel like I'm just hanging on by my fingernails," she sobbed. "What if you weren't hanging on by your fingernails?" I asked. "It's hard to imagine that," she replied.

We talked for a while longer and came up with a plan to address her physical symptoms. I gave her some homework around fleshing out some possible career options, as well.

Laura did her homework and came up with several possibilities for career plans, in fact, she thought up possible Plans B, C, D, and E by the next week when we met. The layoff is a few weeks away, but at least Laura is sleeping better. Having alternate plans in mind and strategies for achieving them were a part of lowering her anxiety. The uncertainty is still real, but she's coping a bit better.

If like Laura, you're hanging on by your fingernails to a job or career, but live in fear of the next layoff or change in the economy, keep reading. Believe it or not, "pushing the reset button" on your life will free you to make whatever changes you need so you have options, no matter what happens.

My favorite professor in business school, Alan Merten, who is now the President of George Mason University, used to say, "The truly successful person is the one with the most good options at any point in time."

This book is about looking at yourself and your career from another point of view and generating some new options. It's a quick and fun read. What are you waiting for?

Chapter

| 3

Five Dangerous Trends That Corporate Leaders Are Ignoring

Bad times have a scientific value. These are occasions a good learner would not miss.

~ Ralph Waldo Emerson

Forget weeping, wailing, and gnashing of teeth. We know there are plenty of things that are suboptimal in the world we live in today. This is a book intended to get you thinking about lots of things: yourself, the world you live in, economic trends that may be affecting you, and most of all what you can do to improve yourself and your life—especially your professional life. The ultimate intent is to get you to take action and quit being complacent. If it's time to "push the reset button on your career" what's stopping you?

As a business and wellness coach, I help my clients to have the careers and work lives they want. As a healthcare professional, I also help my clients to get well, feel well, and stay well. It's too easy to burn out in today's workplace. I call the outcome of the union of business and wellness coaching "*professional competitiveness*." Professional competitiveness is about taking incredibly good care of yourself and your career so you can achieve what you want professionally and stay competitive in today's rapidly changing world.

If what Ralph Waldo Emerson said is true that "bad times ... are occasions a good learner would not miss," what can we learn from what's happening right outside our door today?

I've noticed five trends which are converging to create an employment crisis for many professionals over 40 and many more professionals over 50.

Trend One: The Effect of the Economy on Employment

With the uncertainty in today's economy, many professionals are wondering about the stability of their jobs. Staying employed is becoming a challenge for a significant number of professionals over 40.

The concept of lifetime employment is a thing of the past – It's positively 20th century. It was fine for our fathers' generation who came of age after the Second World War, but for those of us in the generation that came after them, it was definitely not the norm. We may have seen the concept on TV sitcoms, but certainly not in our own careers. Many people grew up expecting lifetime employment because that's what we'd seen in our fathers' careers. Just like we'd seen our fathers come home in time for dinner and work eight-hour days.

Just because you've worked for your current employer for a number of years, it's not realistic to assume you'll end up retiring as an employee of that employer. Nowadays, it seems as though employers are making sure you won't retire on their watch, because you'll cost them too much. It's kind of an evil game of musical chairs where the opportunities keep disappearing the longer you play.

Even though pensions, which like lifetime employment are another relic of the mid-20th century and no longer a cost employers have to control, employers still do have to deal with rising benefits costs and salaries, which can be easily controlled by getting rid of the employees who "cost too much." Consequently, employers seem to be targeting their most expensive employees when they make plans for layoffs.

Layoffs are becoming more and more commonplace. Some companies are cleaning house once per quarter, even when their financial results are acceptable. Companies appear to be targeting costly employees in layoffs. These days, it looks like layoffs are more about cutting costs and not necessarily about performance. Even if your skills are good, there may be less expensive ways for companies to get the same skills, without the extra headcount cost, especially through "outsourcing." This can involve hiring contract employees locally, or overseas.

Many jobs are moving offshore to places where labor is less expensive. American professionals who were used to making a comfortable living by U.S. standards are now finding that they're being offered a small fraction of what they were earning only a few years ago to do the same job as a "contractor."

The flip side of jobs moving overseas, according to those who remain on "global product teams" in the U.S., is that the U.S. workers are working longer days, because they get to participate in early morning and late night teleconferences to stay in sync with their overseas counterparts. The inexpensive workers overseas may be hard-working and may cost less, but their lack of experience and professionalism, coupled with different cultural norms, communication styles, and language skills may make them more difficult to work with.

Working cooperatively between different teams located in different places is a challenging reality of the global workplace. Whether the teams are located in different buildings on the same campus, in other parts of the same country, or on opposite ends of the globe, the kind of effective collegial and casual dialogue required for solving problems is lacking. The remote colleagues are often less accessible, or the dialogues that do occur, happen in meetings rather than informally.

Unemployment is at an all time high in all age groups, but especially for older workers.

According to U.S. Census Bureau statistics from April, 2009, "There was an increase of 120% year over year in unemployed individuals age 55 and older from April '08 to April '09. This age group had the largest jump in unemployment year over year. This equates to [an additional] 1.8 million age 55 and older [unemployed] Americans [in the last year]."[3]

We're finding an increasing number of people over age 40 in the U.S. population who want to work but are unemployed.

Getting Rehired After a Layoff

After a layoff, older workers are taking a longer time to get hired into their next jobs than they have in the past. This in fact may be the real issue. Some have had to recover from multiple layoffs.

Companies are looking for inexpensive labor and energetic, motivated, hard-working employees. Often older workers are perceived as too expensive, or not motivated or hard-working enough. They consistently report having a harder time getting rehired than they experienced earlier in their careers.

Some older professionals hit by layoffs are retraining in order to change careers so they can have more career options and more lucrative opportunities. Others are choosing self-employment.

Career Stalls

For those who aren't being let go, raises are fewer and further between, as are promotions.

Some are stuck in jobs they don't enjoy, which are frustrating, not challenging, or which are suboptimal for other reasons (commute, hours, content, workgroup). However, because they're employed and have significant financial responsibilities, they continue to hang on just to have a steady job.

Trend Two: The Impact of the Baby Boomer Generation in the Labor Market

The Baby Boomer Generation (estimated at over 76 million people in the United States) is now over 40 and rapidly turning 50 and 60. By 2010, the number of workers aged 45 to 54 will increase by 21% and the number of workers aged 55 to 64 will increase by 52%. [4]

After working more than 20 years, these professionals cost their employers a lot in benefits, in addition to their salaries. Older workers' financial responsibilities are also typically greater than their younger colleagues. They may have children in college, aging parents to support, and most likely a mortgage they're still paying down. They may also be aggressively saving for retirement. Most cannot afford to be unemployed, nor do they choose to retire at this point in their careers.

As a result, *the trend toward earlier retirement seems to be reversing*. But it's not only about healthcare benefits and salaries, although, most of the older workers who would like to be employed claim that these factors are important to them.

According to Merrill Lynch's research, many baby boomers plan to be "younger" longer and work longer. Most boomers (65%) will stop working for pay and retire in the traditional sense at some point. However, that phase is more likely to begin in their late 60s. Many surveyed said their ideal work arrangement in retirement would be to "cycle" between periods of work and leisure (42%), followed by part-time work (16%), starting their own business (13%), and full-time work (6%). While 37% of the boomer generation indicate that continued earnings is a very important part of the reason they intend to keep working, 67% assert that continued mental stimulation and challenge is what will motivate them to stay in the game."

Many baby boomers haven't saved enough to kick back full time in retirement and will continue to work to meet basic expenses. But others say they plan to continue working—even if it means cutting back on the hours—because they want to [stay] engaged in their fields."[5]

"Boomer-angs" are people who've retired a few years ago, but due to trends in the financial markets, can no longer afford to be retired. Boomer-angs are re-entering the job market so they can meet their financial obligations now and when they retire once again at some point in the future.

"Today's linear life plan of distinct years for education, work, and leisure is becoming obsolete," the Merrill Lynch researchers concluded. "In its place is emerging a cyclical and phased life plan in which education, work, and leisure exist in different proportions throughout life. Boomers want to work on their terms, doing work customized to their needs."[6]

Research done by Towers Perrin shows that what people who are choosing to work want

"includes competitive health-care and retirement benefits as well as important intangibles like work-schedule and work-location flexibility and respect for employee contributions. Health-care and retirement benefits top the list of what 50-and-older workers at large companies look for … although intangibles like work-life balance, the opportunity to work with high-caliber colleagues, and on-the-job recognition also play significant roles."[7]

AARP's 2003 survey of more than 2,000 workers aged 50-70 sheds light on specific attributes workers 50 and older are looking for in the workplace. "…the most important aspects include:

- An environment in which their opinions are valued and in which they can gain new skills and experiences

- The ability to choose their hours, take time off to care for relatives, and work from home

- An organization that allows people aged 50 and older to remain employed for as long as they want to continue working

- The opportunity to have new experiences and learn new skills

- Access to good health benefits."[8]

Trend Three: The Effects of the Natural Aging Process on the Work Force

There's no doubt that as our bodies age, we experience an impact on our ability to perform optimally in today's high stress corporate work styles. Many professionals over 40 report that they notice having less energy, sleeping poorly, and being more forgetful. The women are also grappling with menopausal and peri-menopausal symptoms.

Others report feeling less motivated and less excited about working at something they're good at but have been doing for 20 or more years. Still others are dealing with chronic illnesses like type II diabetes, hypertension (high blood pressure), sleep apnea, and even cancer and heart disease.

As their bodies age, most people who are used to being healthy, have to learn not to take their bodies and their health for granted. This means mindfully taking better care of their bodies so they stay healthy and age gracefully. Workers over 40 need to make sure they eat three balanced meals a day, get enough of the right kinds of exercise, and/or take supplements daily to stay healthy. They may even have to learn new habits to counteract or help deal with the changes they're experiencing.

Aging bodies may not allow people over 40 to work the long hours they've worked throughout their careers, or their bodies may rebel when they try to continue working the way they've always worked. They may not be able to handle the excesses of coffee, alcohol, athletic activities, sexual performance, or eating patterns from earlier in life as gracefully as they once did.

Aging bodies may demand more sleep, may have trouble falling asleep, or may have difficulty staying asleep. Travelling for business may become more challenging for aging professionals and something they may want to do less of.

Aging bodies may manifest new symptoms that are frustrating: hot flashes, night sweats, low libido, headaches, back pain, arthritis pain and swelling, getting up at night, acid reflux, snoring, and a host of others.

As we age, our bodies become less reliable and predictable. This makes dealing with the daily demands of a high stress professional workplace more challenging than it used to be, and many people feel frustrated that they can no longer live up to their own expectations.

Are baby boomers worried about their health? According to Merrill Lynch's study on baby boomers "The New Retirement Survey": "The unpredictable cost of illness and healthcare is by far Boomers' biggest fear. They are 3 times more worried about a major illness (48%), their ability to pay for healthcare (53%), or winding up in a nursing home (48%) than about dying (17%)." [9]

Rising Healthcare Costs

The graying of the population is only one factor influencing rising healthcare costs.

As a healthcare provider, I find that most people just don't take good enough care of themselves and set themselves up for chronic illnesses; they are accidents waiting to happen. Why don't they take better care of themselves? Because they're too busy making a living, taking care of their families, and staying employed.

A University of Michigan Health Management Research Center study found that: *"Age may be less important than the incidence of specific health risks in driving up health-care costs."*

Essentially as a person's health risks increase, health costs increase. As their health risks decrease, health costs decrease. [10]

Bottom line: *Working professionals need to take better care of themselves* in order to prevent chronic illness and perform optimally at work, so they can keep healthcare costs in check.

Trend 4: The Effects of Years of High Stress

The effects of years of professional stress—hard work, long hours, intense deadlines, coupled with effects of chronological aging—are compounding to create chronic illness and burnout at unprecedented levels.

An evaluation of an aging research survey indicated: "Increased stress is burdening the newer members of the [over 50] age group, rendering them less likely to report vigorous health overall." [11]

Even though baby boomers tend to smoke less and are often thought of as "health obsessed workout fanatics who know their antioxidants from their trans fats and look 10 years younger than their age," [12] when surveyed, they're reporting chronic illnesses such as high cholesterol, diabetes, and hypertension.

The obesity epidemic, which is estimated to affect more than one-third of American adults, [13] certainly includes the baby boomers, which may explain the high cholesterol, hypertension, and diabetes. Even though baby boomers have gym memberships, their desk jobs and non-bicycle commutes make them less active than their ancestors.

According to Daniel Schacter, author of *The Seven Sins of Memory*: "Research on memory loss has indicated that the baby boom generation has been confronted with increasing loss of memory due to the agitated life they lead, which requires that attention is put on many different things at a time. Since older generations were not faced with this rapid life style, and newer generations have lived with this kind of society all their lives, it is said that the baby boom generation was the most damaged one in terms of memory loss due to age." [14]

In case you're wondering what causes memory loss or forgetfulness, usually it's too much stress, not enough sleep, bad nutrition, some medications (e.g. cholesterol-lowering drugs), or often for women, lower estrogen levels.

One physician observed: "I think life is more complicated for someone in their 50s today than someone who was in their 50s six or twelve years ago. There is greater stress, less time to rest, more fatigue, more sleep deprivation." [15]

Life is more complicated for people in their 40s, 50s, and 60s because their bodies are changing, but their expectations haven't. *The people who depend on these folks over 40*, in their families, at work, or in other contexts, *expect them to function as effectively as they did in earlier years when they weren't dealing with declining bodies.* In fact, the expectation is that people in their 50s will help their children through college, help their aging parents, and continue to meet their other family and financial responsibilities, even though their bodies may not have bought into these expectations and may not be as reliable.

Trend 5: Ageism in the Workforce — Layoffs and Rehiring

In recent years, more professionals over 40 have had to deal with the unpleasant realities of ageism. *The talented baby boomer generation is now paying for encouraging others not to "trust anyone over 30."* The baby boomers are now "too expensive," "hard to manage," "culturally not a fit," and all manner of other excuses when younger managers chose not to hire them or decide to lay them off. These days, perhaps the baby boomer watch cry should be, "Don't trust any manager under 40."

This trend should continue to get even more interesting over time since according to AARP:

"From 2006 to 2016, the number of age 55-plus workers is projected to grow by nearly 47 percent, five times faster than the overall labor force." [16]

The AARP also reports, "The number of labor force participants protected by the ADEA (the Age Discrimination Employment Act)— 81 million people aged 40 and older today—is projected to grow to more than 88 million by 2015." [17]

The question is: are they receiving any protection from ADEA?

The U.S. Equal Employment Opportunity Commission reported, "...that *age-related discrimination complaints are at an all-time high*, jumping 28.7% to 24,582 filed in the year that ended September 30, [2008] up from 19,103 in 2007." [18]

According to an AARP Policy & Research report from October 2008, *"a survey showed 60% of workers 45 and older believe that age discrimination exists in the workplace, and 13% say they have personally experienced such discrimination in the past 5 years."* [19]

The youth-oriented culture in today's workplace, which values the latest and greatest in skills and technology, often has no patience for the suggestions and contributions of their older peers or colleagues. These youthful managers may also actively choose not to hire older workers. This is most likely the toughest age discrimination issue- rehiring after a layoff. It's hard to prove and hard to document.

People over 40 are increasingly finding their job searches to be challenging because:

- They are perceived to cost too much
- Their skills may be out of date
- They may be perceived to have health issues
- They may be perceived as not working as hard as younger employees

With these issues in mind, let's look at what professionals over 40 can do to be "professionally competitive" in any economic environment.

Chapter

| 4

How I Pushed the Reset Button on My Career

The Inside Scoop From a Former Marketing Executive and Hiring Manager

Today I'm a licensed acupuncturist and a business and wellness coach. I help corporate professionals "push the reset button" on their careers and their health so they can prevent burnout and have the lives they really want—both professionally and personally.

But it wasn't always that way. By training, I'm an MBA. I spent 20 years working as a high tech professional in Silicon Valley, so I know both the pains and the pleasures of what it's like to work in this culture.

When I first came to California to work in the computer industry in the early 1980s, I was a single parent with a brand new MBA struggling to create as good a life as I could for a small child, while working longer than eight-hour days. I made plenty of sacrifices so my daughter could go to good schools and grow up in a community with other children who had similar values.

I continued to work eight+-hour days even after I remarried and had a second child. Nonetheless, both of my children have been fortunate to have a "village" of good people who guided them well as they grew up with parents who both worked long hours throughout their childhood years.

I love technology, and I enjoyed the challenge of working in growing companies. I enjoyed working with smart technical people who were inventing and implementing, marketing, and selling new products. I was immersed in my work and the years flew by. I achieved my goals, worked for a number of interesting companies, and got raises, stock options, and promotions. My children grew up. And after two decades of constant deadlines, 60-80 hour work weeks, incessant stretch goals, and intense corporate politics, I got pretty fried.

I saw many of my colleagues starting to develop chronic health issues and burnout. I didn't want to go there. It was 2001, and the computer industry tanked. The company I was working for had tanked badly—our lucrative shares and stock options were worth a mere fraction of what they had been. The company was changing in ways I didn't like, becoming more bureaucratic. The things I most valued in the company were all being phased out. What I loved about working there was I could be myself and be valued and respected for my contribution. But at that point, it felt like I couldn't be myself or be valued and respected any more.

Even though I love technology and I had a really exciting job—I was miserable, disappointed, depressed, ill with chronic infections—and the joy was gone. One day I asked myself, *"If you could do anything to make a living, what would you do?" The answer I got completely shocked me.* It wasn't what I was expecting at all. I knew my brain would never come up with an answer like that, so this answer must have come from a source that knew far more about me than I did. Throughout my life, I've been blessed with such insights when I needed them, and I realized that was what was happening. This insight was: "You're done. It's time to do something else."

This got me wondering: what was the "something else" I was supposed to do? Over time, it became clear to me that I needed to take better care of myself, and I realized that my next step was to help my professional colleagues, people like me, do the same.

Since that time, I've become a business and wellness coach, a massage therapist, and a licensed acupuncturist (a primary healthcare provider). I've helped hundreds of high tech professionals improve their careers, reinvent themselves, and live happier, healthier lives.

If I can "push the reset button" on my career and my health, you can too. That's what I'm inviting you to do as you read this book. Whether you decide to continue doing what you've always done with some mid-course corrections, or whether you decide to reinvent yourself, this book is about re-evaluating various aspects of your life and seeing where you can make changes for the long term.

Consider this book the proverbial "grain of sand in the oyster"—an irritation that catalyzes the creation of a beautiful pearl.

5

Pushing the Reset Button on Yourself and Your Career

People always ask me: *What does it mean to "push your own reset button?"*

Think of the electrical or electronic products that have reset buttons. You usually push the reset button on a computer or a trash disposal when everything else you've tried hasn't worked and it's stuck. The analogy to people is clear—we get stuck too. We have pain. We get depressed. We paint ourselves into corners. We get used to doing things in ways that no longer serve us. We get used to seeing situations from one perspective even though there are plenty of other ways to see them. When you push your own reset button, you open up the possibility of resolving what's stuck.

As a coach, a lot of the work I do with clients is to help them get unstuck so they can achieve what they want to achieve, but haven't been able to on their own. I loosen up my clients' assumptions and perceptions by asking powerful questions. I ask them to look at a situation from various perspectives so they can see things differently. Usually my clients gain perspective and self-awareness through this process. They also let go of what no longer serves them, such as negative self-talk, incorrect perceptions, old habits, old beliefs, being stuck, and a host of other issues that keep them from being who they want to be. This allows them to move forward and achieve their goals.

As an acupuncturist, a lot of the work I do with clients is to help get their energy unstuck so they can be free of what ails them. This is another way of pushing the reset button. An acupuncture treatment is a physical reset. It encourages your body to heal itself and correct what's not right. It may unblock blockages, reroute energy in the right direction, clear pathogens, stop pain, or do other healing activities. One day a client came in to her appointment crying, feeling despair. She left my office after the treatment laughing and feeling hopeful. Other clients come in feeling pain and leave pain free. Our bodies have an incredible capacity to heal themselves when we let them—often with a little guidance.

Pushing your reset button is about getting rid of what no longer serves you: pain, illness, depression, limiting beliefs, or false assumptions. It's also about moving forward toward becoming who you want to be and living the way you want to. Pushing the reset button on your career involves looking at several aspects of you and your career, seeing what's working and not working, and making positive changes.

Some people I've worked with have made a few powerful changes, which have made a huge difference. Others have decided to completely reinvent themselves and change many aspects of their professional life. If your career or professional life is causing you pain, just like an acupuncture treatment relieves physical pain, pushing the reset button will ultimately ease your mental and emotional pain and move you into the driver's seat!

Chapter

6

What's Confidence Got to Do With It?

Gaining confidence and staying confident are huge issues whether or not you have a job. When you're between jobs, it often becomes a larger challenge. Any time other people are judging you and can potentially reject you, your confidence is on the line. When your ability to support yourself and/or your family is at stake, it's easy for your confidence to get shaky. When you're facing losing your home, everything you've worked for, even losing your family—believing in yourself is critical.

Confidence is Both About Doing and Being

Doing Confident is your outer confidence, what people see and hear when they're with you. It's your smile, the way you look, your eye contact, your posture, your firm handshake, the way you stand, move, greet people—all the outward manifestations of you. You can often fake outer confidence when you don't feel it, and sometimes faking it is the best you can do. In many instances, you can get away with just doing confident, but for your own sake it's best to both do and be confident.

Being Confident is your inner confidence. This one is harder to fake. It's what people sense about you when they're with you. How do you feel about yourself, your skills, your abilities, your talents, your value, or your life? Being confident is believing in yourself and feeling confident.

What's the magic formula for feeling confident?

I suspect each of us has our own magic formula, whether we realize it or not. Take a moment and remember a time when you felt incredibly confident, on top of your game, bulletproof, successful, as though you'd accomplished something BIG, or completed something you'd struggled with and won. Take a moment and remember how you felt. Feel the feelings you felt at that time, and just enjoy them. That experience and the feelings you felt open the doorway to feeling confident. When you need to access confidence, remember that experience and access those feelings.

Take a moment to look at what you did when you originally felt that feeling of confidence.

How can you do more of that?

Things You Can Do to Promote Confidence

Take good care of yourself. What do you need to do so you can feel and look your best? Be sure to do these things daily.

Remember what you're good at. If you can't, ask five people to tell you what they think you're really good at. (You may be surprised at what they tell you.) Once you know what you're good at, figure out how you can overplay these strengths to your advantage.

Address your weaknesses. Admit to yourself what you could be better at. How could you improve? What could you do this week to take the first step to improve on one of your weaknesses? After you've taken the first step, then take the next step, and keep going until you've made all the improvements you need to. Then to ensure that the improvements stick, create new habits if necessary and get some feedback and support.

Copy someone you think is (both outer and inner) confident. Think of a person you know whom you consider to be very confident. How can you be more like this person (both outer and inner confident)? You can ask this person what they do to feel so confident. Practice being more like this person.

Give yourself challenges and opportunities to accomplish goals—then achieve them. When you stretch yourself even a little and achieve what you set out to achieve, you feel as though you're making progress and you feel proud of yourself. Finish what you start and celebrate your achievements.

Work out regularly. After an intense workout, when your endorphins are coursing through your system, you feel as though you can do anything! Work out regularly so you can reap this and other benefits.

I've noticed that some people seem to find feeling confident a bigger challenge than others. If you're one of these people, cultivate confidence daily by practicing the suggestions above. Better yet, develop your own confidence cultivating tactics and share them on the 5 Strategies Facebook page: http://tinyurl.com/http-facebook5strategies or on my blog http://ninaprice.typepad.com/sharpen/

Chapter

7

5 Strategies for Staying Employed in Today's Economy

Most successful people have not achieved their distinction by having some new talent or opportunity presented to them. They have developed the opportunity that was at hand.

~ Bruce Barton

When life gives you lemons, make lemonade!

~ Lenny Bruce

This book is about what you can do now to develop the opportunity at hand. I believe there's opportunity in everything that happens to us—it's just about how we choose to look at it. If today's economy is giving us lemons—how can we make lemonade?

As I said at the start of this book, whether you're in need of a new job, trying to get back into the job market, secure where you are, or hanging on to your job by your fingernails—this book is for you.

I believe in keeping things simple. I promise to give you very straightforward, concrete suggestions of actions you can take to re-evaluate where you are and what you're doing. Although my suggestions may be simple, it's up to you as to how easy it will be to implement them. Decide now that you'll easily accept the advice offered here, and that you'll commit yourself to systematically reading and implementing whatever you find that applies to you.

To see what is right and not to do it is want of courage.

~ Confucius

All that is necessary for the triumph of evil is that good men do nothing.

~ Edmund Burke

Above all else—take action! All the suggestions I offer are action oriented. You can't make changes or achieve results if you don't take steps to make those changes, so resolve here and now to take action on everything you read that applies to your situation.

Here's a synopsis of the 5 strategies:

Strategy #1 Create a Lifestyle That Makes You a Star Performer

Stress and aging may be the root sources of whatever is causing you not to feel well. It's hard to be a star performer at work when you're not feeling your best. If you want to be a "rock star" at work, creating a lifestyle that supports your health and wellness needs to be your top priority. We'll look at what you can do to have a lifestyle and a work style that best support your top performance on the job (and off the job too).

Strategy #2 Showcase Your Value

Many people believe if you work hard and keep your head down, you will stay employed. While in some cases that may be true, what's most important is that your boss, and his or her boss, know why you're worth what they're paying you. We'll look at what's valued in your company, how to develop your personal brand, and how to be sure others know why having you on their team is well worth it.

Strategy #3 Manage Others' Perceptions of You

Your mirror isn't telling you how others' see you or how they perceive your energy, your behavior, or your professional presentation. Others' perceptions and prejudices can easily affect a hiring decision, your career growth, or even a layoff. We'll look at what you can do to defy stereotypes, impress current and potential employers, and not look your age.

Strategy #4 Reinvigorate Your Relationships and Your Network

You've got plenty of friends, acquaintances, colleagues, and other people in your life who can potentially help you stay employed or get a new job. How often do you stay in touch with the folks in your network? How often do you reach out to help them? Staying employed is often about who you know and how you've cultivated your relationships. We'll explore what you can do to improve your network and to use it responsibly to achieve your goals.

Strategy #5 Get the Job Skills That Are Worth Top Dollar Today

Are your job skills up to date or out of date? Do you know what employers are looking for and requiring of people who do the kind of work you do? Whether you want to stay employed or are looking for a new job, knowing and having the most desired skills will help you be irresistible to your current and/or future employer.

Chapter

8

Strategy #1
Create a Lifestyle That Makes
You a Star Performer

Why Your Health Needs to Be Your Top Priority

It's not stress that kills us, it is our reaction to it.

~ Hans Selye

*Every human being is the author of his own
health or disease.*

~ Buddha

To perform optimally in all areas of your life, and effectively compete against people of all ages, you need to manage your stress and cultivate your health.

The first strategy to staying employed, productive, and professionally competitive in today's economy is to create a lifestyle that supports top performance.

In his best-selling book, *The 7 Habits of Highly Effective People*, Stephen R. Covey tells the classic Aesop's fable of the Goose that Laid the Golden Egg.

A man and his wife had the good fortune to own a goose, which laid a golden egg every day. Although they recognized their good fortune, they soon began to think they were not getting rich fast enough, and imagined the bird must be made of gold inside. They decided to kill it so they could obtain the whole store of precious metal at once. However, when they cut the goose open, they found its innards to be like that of any other goose. They had killed the source of their prosperity!

"Killing the golden goose" has become a metaphor for any short-sighted action that may bring an immediate reward, but will ultimately prove disastrous.

Hopefully the analogy is clear. As our bodies age and as years of high-stress living take their toll on our bodies, if we do nothing to manage our stress and cultivate our health, we too are killing our own golden goose. It's imperative that we do what we can to help ourselves be as healthy as possible.

The reason this is the number one strategy for staying employed in today's economy and achieving professional competitiveness is that when you take care of your stress, your health, your body, your mind, and even your spirit, you have the ability to create whatever you want in life. If you don't take care of them, what's the point of working on the other stuff? You may not be around to enjoy the fruits of your labors!

I hadn't seen my friend Dave for 10 years, and I was thrilled when he attended an open house I hosted at my new office. Dave's in his 50s but he didn't look much older than the last time I saw him. His brown hair was thick and shiny, hardly showing any traces of gray. I was curious about what he was up to and asked about his adventures in recent years. He took my hand, placed it on his chest and said, "Now don't be concerned. I just want you to feel something." It didn't bother me because I'm a massage therapist and Licensed Acupuncturist. I'm used to palpating. Just below his armpit on the edge of his chest, I felt something metal under his skin.

"Wow, what happened?" I asked. I thought it must be a pacemaker—surprising because he looked so healthy. "I had a real wake up call a year and a half ago," he said. "I had a heart attack." It was hard to believe.

Dave is a great guy. He's an IT director with a lovely family and many interests. I didn't think of him as a candidate for a heart attack in his 50s. I was curious about what he thought had caused the heart attack. He said, "It's simple: a sedentary, high stress job, and lots of available fast food." That certainly sounded like a recipe for a heart attack to me. I mentioned that I thought he looked quite healthy now. He said he'd lost 30 pounds and was doing regular workouts to maintain the weight loss.

Are you a health accident waiting to happen?

If you see yourself in the pre-heart attack Dave, what can you change in the next 30 days to create a lifestyle that will better support your success?

You probably know a few things you can change, but keep reading for more ideas.

If you're not feeling well, it's hard to be a superstar.

Staying on top of your game at work is about performing at your best, all the time. You can't really afford to have poor health. And yet there are a number factors that work against maintaining your health, both on the job and in the rest of your life. In addition to the demands of your job, your workplace, as well as your lifestyle, could be contributing to the state of your health.

High Performance Careers

We live in a world of stretch goals and aggressive deadlines, where we feel constant pressure to do better than our previous record. It's all about faster, sooner, and cheaper (better margins), and ideally higher quality.

When it comes to staying healthy, business travel doesn't help! The more you travel for business, the more you're a candidate for the after effects of long plane flights: backaches, sleep deprivation, bacterial and viral infections, and in severe cases deep vein thrombosis. Once you arrive in the remote location, you may also have to deal with the new germs available to you there, and of course adjusting to a new time zone.

Even if you don't do much business travel, the stresses and strains of today's global workplace still affect you. Managers and workers who are part of global organizations are experiencing longer workdays due to schedules designed to accommodate colleagues all over the globe. Many people report that even meetings designed to include all their colleagues don't always prevent miscommunications due to language and culture differences—adding further stress.

The stresses of today's high performance careers are significant and can contribute to the state of your health if you don't do anything to offset them.

What aspect of your professional life most erodes your health? What can you do to offset it so you can maintain your health and perform like a superstar?

High Stress Lifestyles

Although they have to deal with the stresses of a high performance career, most of today's professionals still want to have a life outside of work. Even though they work long hours, most crave a non-work life that is rich and satisfying too.

Juggling Multiple Challenges

The more complex your life becomes, the bigger the juggling act. When you add a home, a family, aging parents, and community responsibilities to a high stress work style, you've got a lot of balls in the air. Keeping them airborne and moving without mishap is not an easy feat. It certainly helps if you have a supportive spouse or partner. Whether or not you have any support, the impact on your stress and your health can be significant.

When things are out of balance in your home or family life, it affects your performance at work. People seem to bring plenty of non-work burdens to the office. Whether it's their pending divorces, their stressful commutes, problems with their teenagers, or issues with their in-laws, their co-workers often feel the effects.

These non-work problems get shared, usually because the person dealing with them needs to vent or needs a supportive, listening ear. Sometimes their co-workers feel the effects inadvertently, because the person with the problem is grouchy or uncooperative at work. Sometimes the person with the problem has an impact on the effectiveness of their workgroup, because they're distracted by their problems and unable to fully contribute on the job.

Limits to Multitasking

We all have limits to what we can do or accomplish given a 24-hour day. Unfortunately, these limits are invisible. Often we don't know that we've hit our limit until something, usually our health, breaks down.

How do you know when you've hit a limit?

My client Emma, a delightful, smiling, energetic woman in her 60s, has had tremendous stress in her life during the last six months. She's the HR director at a company that has had some layoffs. In her position, she's been in charge of all aspects of the layoffs.

She's also seen some significant leadership changes at her company. The CEO retired and an interim CEO took over, causing turmoil in the ranks. High level executives, as well as rank and file employees, were hit in the first layoff, which took place not long after the new CEO arrived. As HR Director, Emma has been dealing with the fallout: people crying in her office sharing their fears and despair and people protesting and complaining. She has been managing the situation professionally. However, she's aware of her uncomfortable feelings about what had to be done and of the impact the stress has had on herself and her co-workers.

In her own group, two of her employees went out on medical leave unexpectedly. Then she had to lay off one of her employees. Her own workload increased significantly, because she couldn't replace her absent employees and didn't have the right people in place to take over the work.

Emma has asthma. Each winter she has at least one incidence of bronchitis. Even though she's had incredible stress in her life for the past six months, she's been getting regular massage and acupuncture treatments to help ease the stress. Because she's mindfully managing her stress and taking good care of her physical and emotional self, she hasn't had any bronchitis or asthma problems! She's amazingly resilient and has been 120% productive during the changes going on at her company.

What do you need to do to better manage your health and stress so you can create a lifestyle that best supports top performance at work?

Many of us are good at taking care of others: our children, our parents, other family members, our employees, even our friends. However, we often forget to take care of ourselves. *One of the best ways to manage stress and cultivate health is to make time to take care of yourself on a regular basis.*

How you take care of yourself is up to you. Ideally it's about proactively addressing areas that need attention that you tend to forget to give attention to.

Here are some ideas for elevating taking care of yourself on your priority list:

Simple things you can do:

1. *Get enough sleep on a regular basis* to rebuild, repair, and revitalize your body's cells. Sleep affects your memory, level of alertness, and your ability to concentrate. Getting enough sleep can reduce the risk of depression and even cancer. When you sleep, you're reducing your stress and any inflammation in your body. Getting enough sleep may even help you lose weight. However, there are plenty of factors in our lives that prevent us from getting a good night's sleep or enough sleep on a regular basis.

    Jet Lag
    Adjusting to a new time zone when you travel can be a challenge for your body. People who do plenty of business travel often find that their performance suffers due to sleep issues while travelling and when they return home.

    Insomnia
    If you have insomnia, you may have trouble going to sleep, staying asleep, or both. If you spend seven to nine hours in bed each night but don't feel refreshed afterward, you could

also have insomnia.

One of the biggest dangers in insomnia is known as the "insomnia cycle." This occurs when a person has difficulty falling asleep one night and then becomes anxious about falling asleep the next night, which makes it more difficult to fall asleep. The more they can't sleep, the more anxious about sleep they become, which keeps them from sleeping.

Here are some common causes of insomnia:

- **Medication Side Effects**: These are especially common with decongestants, some pain relievers, and steroids.
- **Diseases and Health Conditions**: Arthritis, asthma, depression, heart disease, and many other health problems can cause trouble with sleep.
- **Poor Sleep Behaviors**: These include drinking alcohol before bed, exercising before bed, drinking caffeine in the evening, little exposure to sunlight, and other behaviors that interfere with the body successfully achieving enough restful sleep.
- **Sleep Disorders**: Examples are restless leg syndrome or sleep apnea.
- **Stress**: If you can't shut off your mental chatter because you're worried about your complex life, sleep will elude you.
- **Menopause**: Some women experience insomnia when they enter menopause.

Sleep Apnea

If you have sleep apnea, your breathing is interrupted on a regular basis while you sleep. Your upper airway gets blocked when the short tissues at the back of your throat relax too much. The breathing interruptions can happen from five to 100 times per hour. People with sleep apnea don't spend enough time in the deeper stages of sleep. This can lead to moodiness, irritability, and increased risk of accidents. They often wake up repeatedly and briefly during the night. Because of the repetitive awakenings and decreased amount of oxygen in the blood during the sleep interruptions, a person with sleep apnea may also have some of the following symptoms:

- Morning headaches
- Difficulty concentrating
- Problems with memory
- Increased release of stress hormones, such as cortisol (which increases risk for stroke, heart attacks, and other cardiovascular problems)

A great number of people have undiagnosed sleep apnea. If you suspect you could be one of them, talk to your healthcare provider.

Chronic Lack of Sleep

Lack of sleep is an epidemic problem. Some people don't sleep because they have a sleep problem, but others use the quiet hours of the middle of the night to get things done that they can't get done during the day. They could go to bed earlier and sleep more, but they choose not to.

You've probably read somewhere that chronic lack of sleep increases your risk of developing obesity, diabetes, cardiovascular diseases, and infections. It's true. Sleep helps your body stay healthy.

What You Can Do About Chronic Lack of Sleep

Practice good sleep hygiene. Prepare your body for sleep by unwinding and doing relaxing things before bedtime. Here are some suggestions: only sleep and have sex in your bedroom; participate in other activities elsewhere; go to bed and wake up at consistent times; make your bedroom dark; don't smoke; avoid alcohol and caffeine (especially in the afternoon and evening).

Get enough sunlight. Sunlight helps regulate your circadian clock and makes you feel sleepy at night by stimulating your body to produce melatonin (a hormone that regulates your sleep cycle). You need exposure to bright light every day, especially in the morning.

Learn to meditate. Meditation affects the body in exactly the opposite ways that stress does, restoring the body to a calm state, helping the body to repair itself, and preventing new damage due to the physical effects of stress.

When you practice meditation, your heart rate and breathing slow down, your blood pressure normalizes, you use oxygen more efficiently, and you sweat less. Also, your adrenal glands produce less cortisol, your mind ages at a slower rate, and your immune function improves. Meditation helps your mind clear and your creativity increase.

Go to bed earlier. Make getting a good night's sleep a higher priority. This will help you avoid obesity, diabetes, cardiovascular disease, and infections.

2. ***Regularly eat foods that are optimal for your body.*** Learn what the optimal foods for your body are and add them to your menus. With the obesity epidemic in the United States, the good news is that there's no shortage of books or professionals who can help educate you about what your optimal foods are.

3. ***Move your body*** to become and stay fit and prevent your energy from stagnating. If you have a gym membership, how often do you use it? What can you do during your lunch hour, before, or after work to move more?

Caring for your body means moving: walking, dancing, running, bicycling, or whatever you enjoy doing to raise your heart rate and move your qi. We all know that exercise is good for us, but not all of us make it a priority.

If you need to do more exercise, what can you change on an ongoing basis to make it a higher priority?

4. ***Drink water*** to cleanse and detoxify your body. How much water do you drink each day? One client asked whether coffee and Diet Coke counted—absolutely not! Here's why your body needs water:

Water keeps your brain healthy. Your brain tissue is composed of about 85% water. Drinking water regularly keeps the brain functioning properly. Studies have shown that not drinking enough water, or dehydration, can be a key element in causing headaches, migraines, chronic fatigue syndrome, and depression.

Water regulates your body temperature especially during exercise. When you exercise, you lose water by breathing and sweating. As the sweat evaporates, your body cools. Replenishing water loss during exercise is crucial for physical performance and good health. Too much water loss will increase your risk of heat exhaustion. In addition to your normal six to eight cups of water each day, drink a cup before you exercise. Then, for each 20 minutes of exercise, drink another cup or more. Be sure to drink a cup or two after you finish.

Water flushes out toxins. The function of your kidneys is to remove waste from your body. They help to flush toxins such as uric acid, urea, and lactic acid out of your blood stream. These are the toxins that make you feel sluggish and unwell. The toxins can also put a harmful burden on the other systems in the body. Drinking water regularly lessens the burden on your kidneys to keep you pollution free.

Drinking water decreases risk of heart attacks. Researchers found that people who drank more than five glasses of water a day were less likely to die from a heart attack than people who drink less than two glasses.

Water helps raise your metabolism. Metabolism is the means by which the food we consume is turned into energy. The first chemical process that takes place is digestion, which prepares the nutrients in the food to be absorbed by the body and transformed into energy. Drinking plenty of water is essential to maintain good digestion, which keeps your metabolism going. The health benefit of water is better utilization of the nutrients you consume resulting in more energy.

Drinking water helps you to have fresh, healthy skin. Water primarily stimulates the circulation of blood, fluids, and the necessary elements inside your body. Additionally, it controls and regulates the skin's natural balance. When water is warm, it has the power to hydrate, revitalize, detoxify, and oxygenate the skin. Warm water also gets rid of blackheads and makes large pores smaller. Drinking water makes the body more relaxed and invigorated, while it replaces the moisture lost due to everyday activities.

Drinking water helps you lose weight. Some studies have shown that thirst and hunger sensations are triggered together. If there's a slight dehydration, the thirst mechanism may be mistaken for hunger and you may eat when your body is actually craving fluid. As most food contains some water, if you don't drink much, you may be subconsciously driven to eat more to gain the necessary water supply. However, you also gain the undesired effects of increased calorie consumption. Drinking more water can help to prevent overeating and benefit weight loss.[20]

5. *Relax regularly* to regenerate and rejuvenate your body.
    Relaxation can have these health benefits:
    - Relieves stress and mental tension
    - Strengthens your immune system so you're less susceptible to viruses
    - Gives your heart a rest by slowing the heart rate
    - Reduces your blood pressure and cholesterol levels
    - Slows your rate of breathing, which reduces the need for oxygen
    - Increases blood flow to your muscles
    - Decreases your muscle tension
    As a result of relaxation, many people experience:
    - More energy
    - Better sleep
    - Enhanced immunity

- Increased concentration
- Better problem-solving abilities
- Calmer emotions—less anger, crying, anxiety, or frustration
- Fewer headaches and less pain

Relaxation training has been found to widen asthmatics' restricted respiratory passages. In some diabetics, relaxation can reduce the need for insulin. In many patients with chronic, unbearable pain, the training has brought about significant relief.

"Just sitting quietly or, say, watching television, is not enough to produce the physiological changes," said Herbert Benson, director of the Division of Behavioral Medicine at Beth Israel Hospital, a part of Harvard Medical School in Boston. "You need to use a relaxation technique that will break the train of everyday thought, and decrease the activity of the sympathetic nervous system." [21]

Get data and constructive feedback on the state of your health

Annual checkups (or more often if necessary). Get data on what's going on in your body so you can decide how you want to take better care of yourself.

Don't hesitate to consult alternative primary healthcare providers. It's helpful to develop a network of non-allopathic (non-Western medicine) healthcare providers whom you also consult. Their perspectives may offer you new ways of looking at a health issue you have and/or may offer different kinds of helpful solutions.

Make regular self-care appointments (with yourself or with others)

If you don't already make at least one self-care appointment each week, you can choose one of the following, or come up with something else that has more appeal to you:

- Get a weekly massage or acupuncture appointment which can greatly enhance your other stress management activities
- Work with a personal trainer, or schedule regular exercise sessions or classes

- Take a hike with a friend
- Join a sports or cycling team
- Learn a martial art
- Practice Tai Qi or Qi Gong
- Learn yoga and/or meditation
- Schedule regular care for your hair, skin, and/or nails.

Please make sure that you not only make the appointments, but *be sure to keep the appointments*!

What's your favorite way of taking better care of yourself?

Here are some things you can do to be the "Author of Your Own Health" so you can perform like a superstar at work and in the rest of your life:

Notice the factors that could be eroding your health.

Work

- Constant stretch goals or aggressive deadlines
- Business travel
- The stresses and strains of the global workplace
- Other issues

Workplace

- Shared germs
- Ergonomics
- Toxic chemical and hazardous materials
- Toxic people
- • Other issues

Off the Job Issues

- Home
- Family
- Juggling too much
- Other issues

Notice when and how you tend to get sick.

Do you tend to get sick right after you've completed a big project? Or a week before it's due?

Do you tend to get a migraine the day before a big presentation?

Do you tend to get sick every time your children bring something home?

Are you noticing some personal limits you have that you weren't previously aware of?

Have you tackled too much simultaneously at work and at home?

Are there issues in your workplace that are having a bigger effect on you than you realized?

Are you noticing that business travel or another work activity is having an impact on your health?

With your new awareness, what changes can you make to counteract the erosion of your health?

Here are only a few possibilities (I'm sure you'll think of others):

- If you find you're getting sick every time your children bring something home from school or daycare, you may want to look at how much sleep you're getting, what you're eating, and various ways of shoring up your immune system.

- If you notice you get severe repetitive strain issues the week before a deadline, what can you do to prevent this from happening each time?

- If you find you've tackled too much simultaneously at work and at home, take a look to see if there are any tasks you can cut back on or get help with.

The bottom line is that health is the foundation of your ability to live the life you want. Cultivating your health is the single most important thing you can do to create the foundation for your professional success and your ideal lifestyle.

Here's Your Challenge:

Whether you're **between jobs and feeling precarious**, **underemployed** (with or without golden handcuffs), or **hanging on to your job by your fingernails**, please do at least one new activity to take better care of your body during the next month. The more you take care of your body, the more it will be able to support you. Small changes ultimately can have large impacts; all you have to do is take the first step.

Chapter

9

Strategy #2
Showcase Your Value

Remind Your Boss Why You're Worth What He or She Is Paying You

Try not to become a man of success but rather try to become a man of value.

~ Albert Einstein

There should never be any doubt in your boss's mind why you're worth every dime of your salary. Just showing up and doing your work isn't enough. You need to proactively make it clear to everyone you work with through your actions, results, and communication how you add value, ideally to your company's bottom line.

The second strategy to staying employed, productive, and professionally competitive in today's economy is to effectively showcase your value.

If the idea of shameless self-promotion makes you uncomfortable, remind yourself that being unemployed for a long period of time could be more uncomfortable. Seriously, I know most people have been taught not to brag, or they hate being salesy, and some people are just plain shy. Here's an example of a situation I hear about all the time.

Two Billion Dollars Later - Stuck in the Same Place

Renée is in her late 50s. She works for a well-known multinational corporation as a first level manager in marketing. Renée has a first class résumé, incredible judgment, and knows what she's doing. However, when her manager promoted her, he didn't offer her much of a raise and didn't raise her pay grade, so she gets a manager's title, more responsibility, but not much to show for it in terms of career advancement. Renée works hard and consistently delivers excellent results. She launched and managed two billion dollar product lines for the business she's a part of. That's a significant accomplishment. Her manager clearly values her but apparently isn't willing to go the extra mile to support her career advancement. Renée is bothered that others have been rewarded for lesser accomplishments. She's also worried that being the only person over 50 in her group, she could be targeted in a layoff. On the other hand, since she's at a lower pay grade, she may not cost as much as others and therefore may not be a target.

I asked Renée whether she'd talked to her boss's boss. She felt that would be a waste of time. What about the Vice President, how well does she know him? She said she knew him quite well, so I asked her to talk to him. As she suspected, the company had another layoff which Renée survived, but her Vice President had taken on new responsibilities and wasn't available.

Renée's timing is a bit off. Ideally she could have leveraged the opportunity earlier. When the first product line delivered one billion dollars in revenue, she should've been lobbying for more of a promotion and more of a raise. Her results and her value are clear. She's working on high visibility projects that impact the company's bottom line.

Like many people, fear holds her back. She doesn't want to risk losing what she's worked hard for. She's not asking for what she's worth. She keeps her head low and believes that there's no money for raises because that's what her boss is telling her. It's hard to say what kind of a bargaining position Renée is in now. The job market is tight, and she has less ability to move right now, although I suspect if she announced that she had an offer from elsewhere, her management team would not want her to leave. It's hard to say whether they would fight to keep her.

Bottom line: ***Understand your value and the best time to showcase it.*** After a big win is a great time to ask for what you want as long as you understand the politics of the situation.

Sometimes, the only way to get your management's attention is to find another job.

Here's what not to do:

I remember a conversation I had once with a young engineer named Ron who was trying to bargain with me about the salary I was offering him to join my group at a prestigious company. He was technical enough and had experience in the area I needed, so he wasn't going to have a big learning curve. I needed to fill the job soon. I'd offered him what my boss and I considered a fair salary which was more than he was currently earning. My boss was clear that he wasn't willing to offer any more than we'd agreed to and needed me to close Ron.

At that point in time, it was hard to find people who had the technical skills we needed. The people who had those skills usually wanted more exciting technical opportunities. They wanted to work in the hottest, newest areas. The job I had available was appropriate for Ron's skill level, but it wasn't the hottest technology out there at the time. However, there was plenty of opportunity to learn the newer technologies just by coming to work at our company.

Ron kept pushing for more money. I was getting irritated, but keeping my cool. I needed to close him and not lose him. Finally, I simply said to him, "Honestly, from my point of view, you're not worth a dime more to me right now than I'm offering you. Take it or leave it."

In that instance, he demonstrated initiative, but not judgment. He kept making his case but ignored my signals. Nothing he did or said persuaded me through his words or his actions that it was worth a fight with my boss to get him a better salary. It seemed he didn't understand his value to the company, from my perspective.

Did he accept my offer? It turns out, he did.

This second strategy for staying employed in today's economy involves understanding both your own value to your company *and* others' values, for instance those of your boss and your company.

What's Your Value?

To determine your value to your employer (current or future), look at the big picture.

How does what you do for your employer affect the company's bottom line?

Do you make money for your employer?

If you're not in sales, is there something you do that directly influences your employer's bottom line?

If you don't make money for your employer, how can you help your employer to save money?

Another thing to look at is your company's core strategies and strategic projects. Are you working on any strategic projects? Are you implementing a core strategy? If you aren't, how could you?

It's really important to be sure that your work is adding value to the company and that others recognize the value you contribute. Making or saving the company money impacts the bottom line. Implementing core strategies or working on strategic projects advances the company's future.

When you help the bottom line and advance what the company values most, you increase *your* personal value.

What are other keys to establishing your value to your employer?

Here are some suggestions:

- Be sure you *have the skills* to do what your employer needs you to do. (We'll look at this in detail in Strategy #5.)

- *Be sure your work quality is high and consistent.* Even if you think it is, make sure other people, especially your management, agree.

- *Be sure your boss always knows about your results and wins.* It's important that your boss can communicate what you've accomplished to others. When you convey your results and wins to your boss, be sure you do it in a way that makes it incredibly easy for your boss and others to understand.

- *Make sure that others who can promote you, mentor you, or otherwise help you also know about your results and wins.* This may involve documenting what you've done so others can read about it, or showing others your results in the form of a presentation or demo. You could showcase your results on a website, a blog, or an online portfolio and then make key stakeholders aware of it.

- Wherever possible *show initiative*. Go the proverbial "extra mile" to solve a problem or deliver better than expected results. This is where it helps to be genuinely excited and interested in what you're doing. Your enthusiasm, and ideally your results, will be apparent to others: your boss, your customers, your colleagues, and even your detractors.

- *Develop your expertise.* Some people say, "be a 'Go-to Person.'" This means you're the most knowledgeable person about a particular topic, process, customer, competitor, technology, etc. so when others need information, it's clear you're the best source.

- *Develop your own "personal brand."* Your unique promise of value is your personal brand. Not only are you knowledgeable, but you also have a solid track record of predictable results and top performance which has a positive impact on the company.

- *Be visible.* Make sure key players in the company know who you are and what you've done to benefit the company. Keeping your results a secret will not amplify your value.

- *Develop excellent verbal and written communication skills* so you can document what you've accomplished and its impact on the company. When communicating in writing, be both clear and concise, especially in email. When making presentations, be sure you understand how to present the data in the most persuasive way to make your point.

Communicate Most Effectively With Your Boss

You must figure out the best way to communicate with your boss. Find out what he or she needs to know, wants to know, worries about, and cares about. How can you make his or her life at work easier instead of harder? How does your boss prefer to receive information? Does he or she want to receive a status report via email, a one-minute voicemail, a text message, a formal presentation, or a demo? Is it a good idea to also drop by his or her office to talk in person, or would that be considered an intrusion?

Your boss may be inconsistent. You need to be aware of that and have a backup plan. So if you send him or her an email with a question and you get no response, you may have to also send him or her a voicemail or text message encouraging him or her to read that email and respond to you by a certain date and/or time. Or you may have to have a face-to-face meeting and ask directly. This can be challenging when your boss is in a different time zone (literally or figuratively).

One boss I had remarked that one thing he liked about working with me was that when we disagreed about something, it never devolved into an argument or a fight, and it never got personal. Our conversations were based on logical points of view and stayed there. One day, he wondered out loud, whether I could teach his wife to have the same kinds of disagreements with him.

Whether you see your boss every day or once a year, it's really important to keep the information flowing between you. If your boss is an undercommunicator, it's up to you to overcommunicate what you need to know in order to do the best job for him or her.

Ways of Keeping Your Boss Informed:
Cc: your boss on emails
Make sure he/she knows what you're doing (at least weekly):
Status reports or other reports
Regular updates (completions, starting new project)
Group meetings
One-on-ones
Give Your Boss the Information He or She Needs

Here's an example of what not to do:

Ned is a friendly software development engineer at a medium-sized technology company. The people he helps consider him to be knowledgeable and pleasant. He can explain things or help people do technical things with ease. However, it was a different story with his boss. Even though his boss required weekly written status reports, Ned never wrote any. When Ned showed up for group status meetings, or one-on-one conversations with his boss, he was never prepared to share with his boss what he'd accomplished during the last week. Needless to say, his boss found this very frustrating. His boss wasn't seeing a paper trail or the results he was looking for, so he wondered about what Ned was doing all day long.

It appeared to Ned's boss that Ned was helping many people solve small problems but never getting to the larger projects that Ned needed to finish for him. In fact, this turned out to be the case. Ned wanted to be helpful and was indeed helping to solve many small problems, but he never got to his own work.

The boss wondered about Ned's ability to prioritize, and he wondered why Ned wasn't putting his own work first. After months of conversations and various attempts to get Ned to do what his boss wanted, Ned's boss concluded that Ned was ideally suited for a more process-oriented job like technical support or customer support, rather than the project-oriented work of a development engineer. He encouraged Ned to move into a more suitable job.

Ned's unwillingness to provide his boss the information the boss wanted and needed jeopardized their relationship. He was not communicating basic information to his boss, and was failing to deliver the results his boss needed. This caused the boss to distrust Ned, and ultimately manage Ned out of his group.

Trust

The story about Ned demonstrates how crucial it is for your boss to trust you. It's like any other relationship between two people—when you don't trust the other person completely, even though you'd like to, it inhibits what's possible between you. The big difference is that unlike your parents, your children, or your partner, your boss has a very direct influence on your livelihood, your career advancement, and your paycheck.

From the first interview until you move on to your next job, it's crucial to inspire your boss's trust. His or her opinion of you concerning your appearance, your skills, as well as your ability to walk your talk and deliver on time and above expectations, is what will determine how often you get what you want.

You also want to trust your boss. What happens when your boss does something that causes you to distrust him or her?

Blindsided

Annette was a successful sales rep at a large company. She's an active, petite woman in her 50s who has sold technology products to prominent firms for over 25 years. Her track record was solid. She understood how to get things done at the company and was well respected. Two years ago, she decided she needed a change, but wanted to stay with her company. She told her boss she was ready for a change and started informational interviewing with other managers in the company.

She ultimately decided not to move out of her current group and let her manager know she would stay. Her manager surprised Annette by *requiring* her to commit to a full year in her group if she was going to stay; Annette made the commitment. A few months later, when Annette received her annual review, she was horrified. Her manager had given her the worst review she'd ever received. She felt completely blindsided. She talked to her human resources manager and was successful in getting the words in the review changed, but not the grade. A year later, Annette was hit by a layoff.

These days, managers often have the dilemma of having to give someone in their group a bad review. Even if they have an all-star team, someone has to get the proverbial "lump of coal in their stocking" and be ranked as the lowest performer.

On the other hand, it looks like Annette's manager set her up by requiring her to commit to a full year and then by giving her a bad review even though her performance had not changed.

Whether it's an isolated incident or an ongoing "feature" of your relationship, a boss you can't trust is a problem. For many people, it's what causes them to leave a job even when they like the job or the company they work for.

Should you hang in there with a boss you can't trust? Unless you have other more powerful supporters in your management chain, it's probably not a good idea. You need to have the support of your boss and your boss's boss at all times.

Your Personal Brand

As a corporate professional, I had a personal brand before I even knew what one was. I once was interviewing for a job in another part of the company I worked for. The new job was a grade level higher; since I knew I was doing work at a higher level, I wanted a promotion. The hiring manager, an affable guy named Adam, told me during the interview that to be considered for a job at that level, they expected the candidate to have an established personal brand. "You've already established your personal brand in the company, so that wouldn't be an issue," he said. I asked what he thought my personal brand was—I certainly didn't know what it was. I had never heard of a "personal brand" before. Adam's reply was, "If I asked anyone in the top management team of this company who you are, they would know not only who you are, but what you've successfully done to impact the bottom line of this company. You consistently help the company's technical sales force to be more effective in selling the company's products to our customers."

What he was saying was that not only was I visible, but my expertise and results were visible at a high level. The key top level managers at the company knew who I was and what predictable results they could expect from my team and me. My value to the company was clear.

What's the Value of Having a Personal Brand?

- **You're Visible**. People throughout the organization know who you are, including top management.

- **You're A Known Quantity**. People know what to expect. Your results are predictable and of high quality.

- **You're An Expert**. You know what you're doing. Your processes and results have value to the company. People are inclined to pay attention to your communications and recommendations.

What if you're adding value, but no one is noticing?

This is where keeping your boss, and his or her boss, informed about your results and their positive impact on the company is key. "Shameless self-promotion" may even be required.

It could be that what you're doing isn't as strategic as you thought it was. Or you may need to cultivate your relationships with your management team and other decision makers.

What does ethical shameless self-promotion look like?

According to the authors of *Confessions of Shameless Self Promoters,* Jeffrie Story and Debbie Allen, it's all about basic marketing principles: positioning, differentiation, and repetition.

- Align yourself with people who can help you achieve your goals as often as you can. Make it a priority to meet as many people as you can whom you don't already know who can help you achieve your goals.

- Be clear about what's distinctive or memorable about you and amplify it.

- To achieve personal "brand awareness," many people need to see you in the context of what you do that makes a difference, many times. [22]

What if you're not getting the recognition you want for the work you're doing?

This is where it's important to understand what the company values and what your boss values. Often times, when people are working diligently and delivering good results, but no one is noticing, it could be that either what you're doing isn't a high priority for the company, or perhaps it's not strategic to the company's success.

What Does Your Company Value?

Many companies publish their explicit "company values" for the employees to read. Usually the explicit values include profitability, a safe workplace, and quality products and services—basically "motherhood and apple pie" in business terms.

Most companies also have implicit values, which may never be written down but become apparent when you work there. These tend to be elements of the company culture. For example, some companies have implicit dress codes, such as casual dress days on Fridays. Other companies' cultures include 12-hour work days, which they may describe in an interview as a value of "work hard, play hard." Your boss may not insist that you work 12-hour days, but if everyone else does, you may look like a slacker if you don't.

Once you understand what is valued both explicitly and implicitly, then you can decide how you will deliver what is valued.

If the company values people who deliver high quality work by agreed-upon deadlines, and they don't care where or when you work, then you can most likely set the work hours that are best for you and potentially work some of those hours at home. Be sure to keep your boss in the loop so he or she knows what you're up to and when to expect the work you've agreed to deliver.

However, if there's a fundamental mismatch between what the company values and what you value, then you need to decide whether you belong there.

For instance, if your company and your boss value people who meet "stretch goals," and you aren't willing to go the extra mile consistently to achieve the stretch goals that have been agreed to, perhaps you should consider a different company.

If there's a mismatch between what you can do for the company and what they want you to do for them, then you need to decide whether you can learn to do what they want you to, or not.

For example, suppose you've been hired to manage software developers, but your boss needs you to write code as well, due to tight deadlines and being short staffed. If you aren't especially good at coding in the new language that your team codes in, you could be looking at a steep learning curve to achieve what your boss needs done, or you could become a problem for your boss.

Personal Brand Assessment

Expertise

What are you expert at?

What do others consider you an expert at?

Personal Brand

What's your personal brand? (What are you known for?)

What do you want your personal brand to be? (What do you want to be known for?)

What would you need to do to create the personal brand you want?

If I were to ask your boss to tell me what your personal brand is, what would he or she tell me?

If I were to ask your boss's boss to tell me what your personal brand is, what would he or she tell me?

Visibility

How visible are you and your results to your management team?

To the top management of your company?

At what level in your company are you and your brand visible?

Communication Skills

How effective are you in presenting your ideas and persuading others to endorse, support, or sponsor them?

How effective are you in communicating what you've accomplished to your boss and others in your organization?

If I were to ask your boss what you'd accomplished in the last 90 days, what would he or she tell me?

If I were to ask your boss's boss what you'd accomplished in the last 90 days, what would he or she tell me?

If I were to ask your peers what you'd accomplished in the last 90 days, what would they tell me?

Your Value to Your Company

What is the key value you add to your company?

How do you demonstrate your value within your company?

How good are you at articulating to your management team the value of what you do? And to others who benefit from your work?

If I asked your management team what the value of what you do for the company is, what would they tell me?

If I asked others who benefit from your work what the value of what you do for them is, what would they tell me?

Your Value Outside Your Company

What is your key value outside your company to other employers?

If another employer asked you in a job interview to explain the benefits they would get by hiring you, what would you say?

Your Company's Values

What are your company's explicit values?

What are your company's implicit values?

How do you personify your company's explicit and implicit values?

To what extent do the implicit values mesh with your own values?

Here's Your Challenge:

If you're **between jobs and feeling precarious**, what incredible value are you offering a potential employer? How can you present what you have to offer in a way that's irresistible during a job interview?

If you're **underemployed** (with or without golden handcuffs), what can you do to demonstrate or add more value within your company this month?

If you're **hanging on to your job by your fingernails**, consider developing your personal brand. You may even have one and not realize it! Learn to articulate your key value.

Chapter

10

Strategy #3
Manage Others' Perceptions
of You

What Your Mirror Isn't Telling You

First impressions are often the truest, as we find (not
infrequently) to our cost...

A man's look is the work of year; it is stamped on his
countenance by the events of his whole life, nay, more
by the hand of nature, and it is not to be got rid of
easily.

~ William Hazlitt

Whether you're in a job interview, making a proposal, or meeting someone new for whatever reason, you need to manage others' perceptions of you—especially first impressions which have been shown to be the most difficult to change afterwards.

The third strategy to staying employed, productive, and professionally competitive in today's economy is to manage others' perceptions of you.

Before we dive into first impressions, I want to acknowledge that getting feedback about how others perceive you can be difficult because it's very personal. Not only is it very personal, but sometimes it hurts. It often has to do with things you're very sensitive about. Most likely it's a problem you know you have, and it may be a problem you wish or hope others can't see. Usually they do, especially during a first impression. Occasionally what others see during a first impression is a complete surprise to you when you find out about it; and you feel very judged, even blindsided.

I bring this up because like you, I don't always enjoy this kind of feedback . I've learned from others who welcome feedback that it's often better to get the feedback from someone who cares about you and your success before others judge your for it. Then you can decide if and how you'll address the issue before you deal with the judgment that can come when you meet someone important at a job interview, key presentation, first date, etc.

I remember the time a friend of mine invited all her women friends over for a Friday night makeover party. About 20 or 30 women attended. Most of us were young mothers. Carole, the woman who did the makeovers, was one of our friends. She was a model and very beautiful. She always looked "perfect," even when she was nine months pregnant. Not one strand of her blonde hair was ever out of place, her clothes always looked freshly ironed, and her makeup was never smudged. At the makeover party, Carole gave each of us who wanted one, a private makeup consultation. During my consultation, Carole gave me some suggestions about things I could do to improve my makeup. At the end of the consultation she said to me, "You know, Nina, the one thing you need to do that would make you look so much better would be to just lose some weight."

I suspect you can imagine how I felt—hurt, angry, judged, and put down. I thought to myself: you make it sound so easy, but you clearly have never struggled with losing weight.

Perhaps you've had a similar experience where someone has offered you obvious, well-meaning advice, but for whatever reason it's something that's hard for you to fix. Or else it's something you're really sensitive about, because it's a problem that's bothered you for a long time.

Pushing the reset button often has to do with looking at our "blind spots." Looking at what gets in our way. Looking at the "bad breath" issues that keep us from getting what we want. Looking at what we've struggled with. Ideally, pushing the reset button allows you to let go of what no longer serves you—the old stories, the old self-image, the old beliefs. It's about letting go of the struggle and dealing with the issue once and for all. It's about creating new beliefs, new habits, and new ways of seeing yourself so others can see you that same new way.

Pushing the reset button can also be about looking at a new issue, perhaps one that has to do with aging. One that never used to be a problem, but now is getting in your way. It may also have to do with dealing with other people's stereotypes and values—what's acceptable, what's beautiful, what's "normal," what's "appropriate," what's valued.

It's amazing how many of these "blind spots" and "bad breath" issues show up during a first impression, because the people who are meeting you have no history with you; they just see what you present to them—warts and all.

My request to you is that you check your ego, insecurities, hurt, anger, frustration, fear, and the rest of your feelings at the door. When you get feedback from others ask yourself:

- What's the gift here for me?

- How can I use this information to become a better (more attractive, more hireable, more efficient, more desirable…) person?

- What's the ugly truth that hurts so much?

- What's the real truth?

- What do I need to do about this feedback in order to become who I want to be?

- What do I need to do about this feedback in order to achieve what I want to achieve?

First Impressions

What if you were clairaudient, someone who could hear exactly what the person across the table from you is thinking about you while they're interviewing you for a job?

What would the interviewer be noticing? Would the interviewer notice that you forgot to brush your teeth this morning? Or how grey your hair is? That you're overdue for a haircut? That your socks don't match? Or what about the 20 extra pounds you're carrying? Or that your shirt wasn't ironed? Would the interviewer notice how tired you are and that you look like you haven't slept well for days?

Hopefully, your interviewer was so dazzled by your expertise and excellent insights that he or she either didn't notice or wasn't bothered by these distractions. But what if he or she noticed most or all of them?

Other people's first impressions of you are crucial to whether they want to continue to consider you, your ideas, or your solutions, especially in a job interview. If they're enthralled with your appearance, but don't think you know what you're doing, that could be the proverbial "kiss of death" to your chances of getting the job. Your mission during any job interview (as well as once you're hired) is to overdeliver on the value your potential employer is looking for, and build the foundation for an ongoing relationship.

Minimize Distractions

Meanwhile, you also want to minimize any distractions. A *distraction* is anything that captures another person's attention and blinds them to your real talents and expertise. Whether it's hair in the wrong places, a sweaty palmed handshake, inappropriate dress, an arrogant demeanor, or an absence of rapport or energy in the conversation—beware! Some people will be put off by these things and won't give you the benefit of the doubt, or a second interview. Chalk it up to chemistry. If you've gotten a first in-person job interview, why risk jeopardizing an ongoing relationship due to a distraction?

Job Interviews: the ultimate in first impressions

Job interviews and first dates are probably the ultimate first impressions. A serious part of your life could be affected by the outcome. Treating a job interview like a first date is not a bad idea; the converse is also true.

Here are some practical guidelines for managing first impressions that count:

Do some homework: be prepared

- Research the company's history, financials, products, and culture.

- Be clear about what information you want to learn about the company, what it's like to work there and the specific job you're interviewing for.

- Check out the company's website and read it thoroughly.

- If you can, talk to someone who currently works for the company to find out what's valued at this company. What's important to the leaders? How influential is the group that you're going to talk to?

- Have a list of questions prepared to ask during your interview(s).

Be aware of others' perceptions and stereotypes

Consciously avoid distractions. Get feedback from an objective person several days before the job interview about how you look and what messages you're sending both deliberately and inadvertently.

Prepare for your interview by addressing simple things like hygiene, hair, skin, and nails on an ongoing basis. Make it a habit to look your best at all times. Think through the other possible distractions: get a haircut and/or dye your hair, get rid of extraneous hair, press your shirt, make sure your interview clothes are clean, and wear socks that match.

If you need advice on your appearance from a professional, don't be shy to ask someone, even if you're a guy. I used to think the idea of working with an image consultant was unnecessary, until I worked with one and saw the benefit. Image consultants can help you fine tune your appearance so you look terrific. When you want to make the best first impression, you want to look amazing—nothing less. Looking great means looking authentic—like yourself at your best.

When you're dealing with people's stereotypes about older workers, looking your best could mean the difference between getting a job and not getting a job.

You never know what the person across the table from you at an interview sees when they look at you. Hopefully, your interviewer is capable of seeing the value you bring to the job you're interviewing for and not just your flaws. Many interviewers are capable of seeing this value, but many are not. The trouble is that in today's economy, you're most likely competing against many other people for every job. You can't afford to distract your interviewer, and you have no idea what stereotypes, values, and attitudes could be lurking in that person's head.

Bottom line: Do your best to understand the stereotypes, values, and attitudes your interviewers may have, and then proactively defy the stereotypes with your appearance, your behavior, and your words.

Understand the values of the organization or individuals you're meeting

<u>*Be on your best behavior*</u>

- Be punctual

- Have impeccable manners

- Build rapport with those who interview you by matching and mirroring their behavior and speech

<u>*Understand the "uniform" and dress accordingly*</u>

Understand the dress code for the company and for the functional area. If you're interviewing for a job in finance, don't dress like a software engineer. This isn't the time to show your "out there individuality." Build connection by developing rapport with those who interview you by dressing similarly to the way they do when you go to interview with them. Grooming is also very important. Just because the uniform is casual doesn't mean it's okay to slack off on your grooming.

How Not to Look Your Age

My client Vic had always planned to retire at 55. He was unexpectedly hit by a layoff at 51. He still had one son at home and two in college, so he really couldn't afford to retire at this point. Even though he had an excellent résumé, he wasn't having much success getting a new job. When I met and talked to Vic, I knew why. Even though Vic was in his early 50s, he looked much older. His hair and skin looked neglected, and his clothes were out of date. His energy level was lower than I expected for someone his age, and he needed to lose a few pounds. I did a quick health evaluation, and we discussed some things he could be doing to take better care of himself. Most of all, I thought he needed a "makeover."

I know that most of my male clients are a bit resistant to getting a "makeover," but Vic *really* needed one. I told him about the successes some of my other male clients had in getting job offers after paying attention to the appearance of their hair, skin, and interview clothes. Even though he was a bit resistant at first, with his wife's encouragement, Vic agreed to get some insights from professionals that I hand picked. I had Vic consult a hairdresser, an aesthetician, and an image consultant.

The hairdresser offered him several options. Since he's fortunate to still have more hair than most men his age, he could either leave his hair grey, he could do grey reduction, or he could color his hair to match his non-grey hair. Vic chose grey reduction, which he felt would look most natural.

From the aesthetician, Vic learned how to help his skin look healthier and younger. He also let her wax some extraneous hair. The image consultant went shopping with him and helped him find two sets of attractive interview clothes. When I next saw him, I was thrilled. He looked terrific and he enjoyed his new look! His wife called to thank me for suggesting the makeover—she was also thrilled with the results.

On his own, Vic decided to start a more regular workout program. He lost some weight and his energy level was better. We did some practice interviews, and in a month he had more than one job offer. Vic was back in charge of his professional life.

Do You Look Your Age? Really?

Hair

Even if you like your current haircut, get some feedback from a professional (an image consultant or a hairdresser) about your hairstyle.

- Is it appropriate for you?
- Is the style up to date or out of date?
- What other cuts are options for you?
- Would you look younger with a different haircut?
- Does your hair look too grey?
- Should you consider grey reduction or hair dye?
- If so, what color would look most natural given your skin tone?
- If you don't have much hair, would you look younger with a shaved head?
- Do you have extraneous hair (hair in the wrong places)?
- If so, what's the best way to manage or get rid of it?

Skin

Both men and women need to pay attention to their skin after 40. Consult an aesthetician and have them recommend products that are appropriate for your skin type.

- How dry or oily is your skin?
- Do you have wrinkles?
- Blemishes?
- Skin cancers?
- What's the best thing for you to do about them?
- What does the aesthetician recommend as a routine for skin self-care to promote healthy, young-looking skin?

Energy

Your energy level and enthusiasm are very important to how others perceive you. Pay attention to maintaining a positive, enthusiastic outlook with plenty of energy to amplify it. Ask your image consultant for feedback on your energy and enthusiasm.

- What can you do to maintain as high an energy level as possible?

- Are there ways you could dress or present yourself that would enhance others' perception of you as an energetic, enthusiastic person?

Fitness/Weight

Regular fitness activities can improve your energy level and the fit of your clothes. If you're not doing a regular workout, what can you do to enhance your fitness and appearance of fitness? What are you *willing* to do to improve your fitness? Consult a personal trainer and get some suggestions about what you could be doing, and consider hiring one to get you started.

Often, the easiest way to look younger is to lose some weight if you're carrying extra pounds. Losing the weight will undoubtedly benefit your health and your appearance. Consult a nutritionist for insights as to the optimal foods for your body type, and develop a way of eating that you enjoy and that will deliver the (permanent) weight loss results you're looking for. If you've lost weight before but haven't been able to maintain your weight loss, get some coaching on how to most effectively maintain it.

Clothing

How you dress, how you look in your clothes, and what your clothes say about you are all important to how others perceive you. Ask your image consultant about what styles of clothing will make you look most youthful, attractive, and professional. Style and fit are important. It's also important to look up to date and in sync with what your co-workers are wearing. Be sure you know the "uniform" for the type of work you want to do and that you look good in the uniform.

An Attitude of Confidence

Everything about your appearance, speech, and behavior needs to project confidence. Even your teeth and your nails will be subject to scrutiny. Make sure your teeth are clean and unstained and that your nails look well groomed (i.e. not bitten and uncared for). Check your posture and your gait. Make sure they enhance your appearance.

Be sure you're prepared to be interviewed by people who may be younger than you. You may even have a group interview. Regardless of what is said during the interviews, be unflappable and keep your energy up.

Ageism is About Stereotypes

Once you've addressed the visual and energetic stereotypes, it's time to look at some of the conceptual stereotypes about older workers and figure out how to defy these.

Here are some common stereotypic perceptions about older workers:

- Their skills are obsolete
- They're ineffective
- They're expensive
- They don't work as hard
- They're not as motivated
- They're difficult to manage
- They're not as healthy

Now that you understand the stereotypes, how will you actively or proactively defy them?

Incompetent/Obsolete Skills/Ineffective

Be sure you know what skills are valued at this company, ideally by the manager and members of the workgroup you're interviewing with.

Do you have the skills they're looking for?

How good are you at using these skills?

Have you already used these skills on the job elsewhere?

Position yourself as a lifelong learner and demonstrate it by taking classes and learning new skills.

Be sure you've done your homework on this company and this industry. What are the trends and issues this industry in general and this company in particular are facing?

What results or wins have you created that this employer would be interested in? Be sure you have concrete examples.

What value are you offering this employer? How will you articulate and demonstrate your value?

If you've worked for a long period of time at your previous employer, the hiring manager will most likely wonder how well you deal with change or how well you'll be able to adapt to a new corporate culture. Be prepared to answer such questions.

A good way to be perceived as up to date is to be tech savvy. If you haven't already, build some appealing social media profiles for yourself and get active on social media websites (see the bonus chapter in this book for how to do this). Write a blog which showcases your expertise, and then link your blog to your social media pages. You can also write articles to showcase your expertise and post them on article directories like http://www.ezinearticles.com.

Expensive

Consider what the salary range is for this job. Is it acceptable? If not what would be acceptable?

Do some research. What do other people in your field make? Check out salary surveys. Be clear about what your acceptable salary range is.

In your cover letter and during interviews, be clear about what besides your salary motivates you. Salary is always negotiable. *Your past salary isn't important.* The salary you negotiate with your new employer should reflect your skills, your experience, and what you can do for the organization. Once again be clear about the value you're offering your potential employer.

Don't Work as Hard

Be sure you understand this company's implicit values. If working 12-hour days is the norm and you want to work less than 12 hours a day, that could hurt you. Make sure your values match those of the companies you talk to.

If you'd rather work fewer hours than an employer wants you to, you may want to reconsider looking for a "full-time job." Perhaps you'd be happier as a contract employee where you can have a more flexible schedule.

These days, many older workers are being offered contracts rather than full-time employment. For many people, being employed is better than being unemployed, and they're willing to accept a contract offer.

Be open to a contract if that's what's offered, especially if you like the company and the others you'd be working with.

Not as Motivated

Focus on the value the company will get when they hire you. Be prepared to tell stories that showcase your results and your performance. Be clear about how to show your motivation with specific recent examples.

How motivated are you? Some people report that after doing the work they've done for over 20 years, they're experts and are really good at what they do, but aren't as motivated as they were when they first started their career. Is this true for you?

Might it make sense for you to repackage your skills and offer what you're good at in a new context that might be more interesting to you?

- Could you teach or coach others to be more effective or expert at doing what you do? (e.g. experienced sales person teaching sales skills to new sales reps)

- Could you do what you're good at in a company in another industry? (e.g. selling a different kind of product to a different industry)

- Could you do what you're good at in a different department? (e.g. engineering project manager working as an IT project manager)

- Could you take a different role within your functional area, perhaps one you've done some years ago? (e.g. product manager working as an outbound marketing manager)

- Would you take an individual contributor role after having being a manager? (e.g. software development manager working as a software engineer)

Difficult to Manage

Younger managers often find older employees "difficult to manage" or they fear they will be. Be sure to build rapport and connect with your interviewer. Find out what you have in common and emphasize that.

Younger managers may find an older employee who appears to be a "know it all" to be difficult to manage. Beware of "know it all" behaviors and language.

Flexibility, loyalty, patience, and willingness to be a team player are all considered to be important assets of older workers. If your prospective employer values these characteristics, it helps to emphasize them and have past accomplishments that illustrate them.

Not Healthy

Looking and being fit is the first step towards appearing healthy. This is where good grooming and care for your hair, skin, teeth, and nails will pay off. If you do have a visible health problem, what can you do to minimize its visual impact?

Understanding the stereotypes that younger managers may have and their fears or issues around hiring an older professional into their group, gives you additional help in positioning yourself as the ideal candidate in a job interview. Anticipate the issues, and plan what you will say to advance yourself as the best candidate.

Seeing the Real Value

When it comes to first impressions, I tend to give most of the people I meet the benefit of the doubt. As a hiring manager, I hired some incredibly talented people who my peers would never have considered. I hired people who were changing careers, who pursued alternative lifestyles, who "looked unusual," who other managers had given up on, and who just needed a chance to prove themselves in a high tech company. In the end, all of these hires were successful. In fact, one of my least successful hires was someone who had the exact skill qualifications for the job, but lacked the resourcefulness to work effectively in the environment. The people I hired were talented. I knew they were resourceful enough to do the job I needed done, even though their résumé might not have been a perfect match for the job.

In fact, I remember a couple of times having to convince my boss to trust my perception of the right person to hire. Usually, it was because the person I wanted to hire was in some way not what my boss had in mind.

I was working in an organization that had trouble retaining employees. They had a bad reputation and were in a turnaround mode. I inherited a team which had lost a lot of people, and my boss wanted me to hire between five and ten superstars to reinvigorate the group within a matter of months. The year was 2000 at the height of the Internet boom, and there just weren't a lot of people available to hire. I successfully hired seven people for my group in a matter of months.

Anne had worked with me at a previous company. I knew firsthand that she produced superstar results. She went through the interview process with my group and another group at our company. She told me honestly that she preferred the job that the other group had to offer to the one I was offering. I still wanted to hire her for my group. My boss liked her. All I needed was the signature of my boss's boss Ed on her offer letter.

Ed was the person who had convinced me to take my job. I'd worked with him before and thought he was outstanding. He was also a friend. For some reason, though, he dragged his feet about signing the offer letter. I really wanted to close the offer and get Anne on board before the other group made her an offer. I could tell he was having trouble with Anne. I talked to some people and finally figured out that his hesitation had to do with Anne's weight. She probably weighed more than 300 pounds. I had a heart-to-heart chat with Ed and persuaded him that he wouldn't regret signing the offer letter for one minute. Ed finally signed the offer letter, and some time later he apologized to me for doubting my choice. Anne has gone on to be a superstar at the company, and she still has a great relationship with Ed, whom she worked for in several different groups after the initial one with me.

The truth is that most hiring managers aren't going to look past the physical reality that you present to them, so it's your responsibility to be prepared.

Do your homework:

- Find out about the company and the group that's interviewing you.

- Be clear about what you want to find out from the interview.

- Be prepared for many kinds of questions: job-related, how you've handled situations in the past, skill-related, industry-related, even questions that may seem out of bounds.

- Know how others perceive you, and be prepared to answer their concerns, even proactively.

- Understand potential stereotypes that your interviewers may have, and be prepared to defy them.

- Look terrific.

- Present yourself well.

- Practice, practice, practice before the interview.

- Get feedback, and remember to listen for the "gift" to you in the feedback; make adjustments based on the feedback.

Here's Your Challenge:

If you're **between jobs and feeling precarious**, spend time researching companies or opportunities you're interested in. Many experts say that today's job seekers don't feel as confident as they could, because they don't do adequate preparation for their interviews. To be sure you're prepared—practice preparing!

If you're **underemployed** (with or without golden handcuffs), or **hanging on to your job by your fingernails**, treat yourself to some feedback on how others perceive you. Once you know what you could improve, take the first step to improving it!

11

Strategy #4
Reinvigorate Your
Relationships and Your
Network

It's All About Who You Know and Who Knows You

It isn't just what you know, and it isn't just who you know. It's actually who you know, who knows you, and what you do for a living.

~Bob Burg

Position yourself as a center of influence – the one who knows the movers and shakers. People will respond to that, and you'll soon become what you project.

~Bob Burg

The people you know can offer you insights, information, contacts, opportunities, recommendations, and job leads. You know more people than you realize, and you have access to even more people than you already know. Reinvigorate your network to access its benefits and valuable relationships.

The fourth strategy to staying employed, productive, and professionally competitive in today's economy is to reinvigorate your relationships and your network.

You'll want to do this with people you work with directly and others with whom you have professional dealings. Professional competitiveness isn't just about what you know; it's also about who you know. No matter your education, job title, or level of experience, maintaining and cultivating a professional network is vital to staying employed, getting hired, and being effective on the job.

Your professional network is comprised of the people you know: people you work with now or have worked with in the past. These are your colleagues, your bosses, your peers, your direct reports, and vendors and salespeople who've sold you products or services. I'm sure you've also met people through professional organizations or volunteer work. You probably know people in your community: neighbors, people from church, the PTA, your children's friends' parents, people who've coached your children's sports teams, or those who lead scout troops. You can also include your relatives and friends, and even friends of your relatives and friends. All these people are part of your network. Each of them can potentially be of help to you, and you can potentially be of help to them.

Perhaps you're good at staying in touch with your network. Maybe you send yearly Christmas or birthday cards. Perhaps you occasionally have a meal together or invite them to your annual party. However, many people forget to stay in touch with their network, or they only contact their network when they're looking for a job or need something else from them.

The best time to cultivate your network is when you don't need their help

Experts say that the best way to approach people in your network is to show interest in them and what they need. What better way to be a friend? Most people like to help others, and when you stay in touch, you can often find ways to show interest and be helpful.

Regular interaction with people in your network has many benefits. You can find out what they're up to professionally or personally. Perhaps they're working for a hot new startup company or developing an interesting new technology. Maybe they've gone back to school to prepare for a new career, or they've been honored with a research fellowship, or maybe they're taking an executive MBA program. Perhaps they've been transferred overseas or their spouse has, so they're spending time living abroad and travelling. Maybe they've made a career change and have become a venture capitalist or a consultant. Could be they've retired to do day trading. Any of their changes could represent opportunities for you or could offer you new information.

Regular interaction with your network might mean that you get invited to some interesting events like family celebrations, charity events, political fundraisers, weekend getaways, or parties. Any of these are possible opportunities for you to meet people you don't know but might want to know.

Other benefits to regular interaction with your network are:

Deeper friendships – The more experiences you have with people in your network, the greater chance you have to cultivate deeper friendships. Sometimes, you may discover that people you already know well are better able to help you than you thought.

Access to people you'd like to meet – Your friends may know how to get you introduced to people you'd like to meet and talk to.

New contacts – Your friends may think of people you should meet who may turn out to be helpful to you.

New information:

- About your industry
- About what's happening in other companies
- Salary information
- About hot new technology
- About up-to-date job skills
- What mutual friends are doing
- Where mutual friends are working

- New companies you may be interested in

Here are some suggestions for expanding your network or taking it to the next level:

- Broaden your professional circles; reach out to a diverse socio-economic group of people.

- Volunteer to speak at local conferences or events related to your area of expertise.

- When you present to groups and share your knowledge, you establish yourself and your expertise in your professional community.

- Participate in forums, mailing lists, and other online communities where you can become recognized as an expert in your field.

- Write your own blog, and/or guest write for someone else's blog. Pick topics that demonstrate and articulate your expertise. Be opinionated to get noticed, but above all be professional.

- Sign up at sites like LinkedIn and Twitter to meet people in your field with whom you share interests. Help them whenever possible. Be active in social networking groups by sharing your ideas, commenting on others' posts, and connecting and reconnecting with others.

- Non-profit organizations always need help. Approach them and ask if there's anything they need done. Use volunteer opportunities to hone and practice new job skills you've learned. You'll also meet new people while you're adding value in your community through this volunteer work.

- Put other people's needs ahead of your own when networking. When you help the people you meet, they'll be more inclined to help you, and others will be more inclined to help you. Professionals who habitually facilitate introductions earn goodwill and reputations as valuable resources and colleagues.

Professional networking can be enjoyable, especially when approached with sincere curiosity. It's about meeting people within your industry, sharing your knowledge, marketing yourself, and showing people why you should be the one they look to for help.

My client Bart knew many people in his field and in his industry but after talking to him, it was clear that *he didn't keep up his relationships.* He'd stay in touch once in a while but not on an ongoing basis. I challenged him to do a better job of managing and working his network. I also gave him what I call "the LinkedIn challenge."

Social networking adds a powerful tool to cultivating and nurturing your business network. It gives you a simple, yet effective way to casually stay in touch with the colleagues you value and a chance to meet others whom you admire or might like to work with in the future.

LinkedIn (http://www.LinkedIn.com) is a social network for corporate professionals, which extends worldwide.

Facebook (http://www.Facebook.com) is also a helpful social network, which more corporate professionals are joining.

Both are worth investigating if you haven't already done so. (See the bonus chapter in this book for how to get started with social networking sites.)

Nina's LinkedIn Challenge:
1. Put up your detailed contact information on LinkedIn.
2. You can even use LinkedIn as an online résumé.
3. Then invite everyone you know to become a connection on LinkedIn.
4. You can also invite people you respect whom you've worked for, and worked with, to write you recommendations.

Here's what you'll find when you start social networking:
- You'll discover that you know more people than you realize.
- You'll be surprised by the number of people you'll reconnect with.

- You'll be amazed at the recommendations people write for you.

One of my clients, an engineering manager at a well-known Silicon Valley company, told me that when he's hiring someone, rather than ask for references, he goes to the person's LinkedIn page and finds someone they know in common. Then he phones their common connection and does an informal reference check. He finds that he gets more useful information that way.

Another person at one of my workshops told me she makes it easy for recruiters to find her through LinkedIn by mentioning in her profile that she's looking for a job doing Enterprise software sales.

Bart accepted my LinkedIn challenge and did an amazing job connecting to 25 years worth of colleagues all over Silicon Valley.

His results were magical:

- He had lunch with friends he hadn't seen for years and was happy to get reacquainted with them.

- His friends found out that he was looking for a job and knew his skills. They sent him plenty of leads to appropriate jobs. They also introduced him to helpful contacts.

- The people who wrote recommendations for him did a great job of endorsing him and his work.

As a result of a recommendation from a very influential technologist, Bart got an email from a person he knew of, but didn't know well. That person said that if the influential technologist had endorsed Bart so highly, he needed to meet him and talk to him about an opportunity with his company.

Bart followed up on all the leads and contacts. He finally found a suitable job, which allowed him to learn the skills he felt he needed to learn while leveraging proven skills and industry knowledge he already had.

After starting his new job, Bart is continuing to manage and work his network. He's very conscientious about staying in touch with the colleagues who helped him and those he met through the process of finding his job. He now realizes the power of his network and that he needs to stay in touch with what's happening in the industry, especially through the eyes of the colleagues he trusts.

Bart now uses LinkedIn on a regular basis to communicate with his colleagues. His experience with LinkedIn gave him several powerful benefits:

- Reconnecting with former colleagues
- Job leads
- Recommendations
- A tool for ongoing communication with his network

Bart plans to stay in touch even when he's not looking for a job. He can also help others who are looking for jobs through sharing contacts and information he has.

And I've encouraged him to join professional groups on LinkedIn to meet others with similar skills and interests. He can find out about events and conferences he may want to attend. He can share information such as posting leads about jobs available at his company to groups of people who may be interested.

I'm giving you the LinkedIn challenge too. See what happens. Social networking is incredibly powerful. If you haven't already, please invite me to be one of your LinkedIn connections.

Remember: the best time to grow and cultivate your network is when you don't need to (i.e. when you're not looking for a job and don't need a recommendation). In that way, when you do need to ask a favor, ideally you'll have already done something to help the person you're contacting.

It's vital to keep your network alive, especially when you don't need it. Be sure you communicate to the folks in your network how much you value them and that you're there to help them too.

Action step

How effective is your current network at:

- Offering you helpful information
- Providing job leads
- Recommending your work

- Introducing you to others you would like to meet

Who do you know and who knows you?

- People you work with directly: your boss, your peers, your customers, your colleagues
- Other people at your company
- People you've worked with in the past
- People you know through professional organizations
- People in your community: neighbors, people at your church, parents of your children's friends, acquaintances
- Friends, relatives, friends of friends and relatives
- Who's in your network now?
- Who would you like to add to your network now?
- What can you do during the next 30 - 90 days to reinvigorate your network?

How can you meet the people you need to know in order to do what you want to do next?

<u>Here's Your Challenge:</u>

Whether you're ***between jobs and feeling precarious***, ***underemployed*** (with or without golden handcuffs), or ***hanging on to your job by your fingernails***, please take at least one action to grow or cultivate your network during the next month. The more you do this, the more your network will be able to support you when you need support. Remember, the best time to grow and cultivate your network is when you don't need support.

12

Strategy #5
Get the Job Skills That Are
Worth Top Dollar Today

Be Irresistible to Your Current and/or Future Employer

*Your earning ability today is largely dependent upon your knowledge,
skill and your ability to combine that knowledge and skill in such a way
that you contribute value for which customers are going to pay.*

~ Brian Tracy

*Everybody has talent, it's just a matter of moving
around until you've discovered what it is.*

~ George Lucas

To achieve professional competitiveness, it's key that you have the
skills employers are seeking and willing to pay top dollar for.

The fifth strategy to staying employed, productive, and professionally competitive in today's economy is to get the job skills that are worth top dollar today.

The Ant and The Grasshopper (another of Aesop's Fables)

One summer's day, a Grasshopper was hopping about, chirping and singing to its heart's content. An Ant passed by, bearing an ear of corn he was taking to the nest.

"Why not come and chat with me," said the Grasshopper, "instead of toiling in that way?"

"I am helping to lay up food for the winter," said the Ant, "and recommend you do the same."

"Why bother about winter?" said the Grasshopper. "We have plenty of food now."

The Ant went on its way. When winter came the Grasshopper had no food and found itself dying of hunger, while it saw the ants distributing corn and grain from the stores they had collected in the summer.

Moral: Prepare for the future.

What Skills Are Employers Looking for Today?

The New Realities

Today's global, more technical workplace is requiring new skills and new ways of doing things. Here we'll look at four scenarios in today's workplace and the crucial skills required for each. First, we'll look at the virtual teams in today's global workplace where progress is made even while some members of the team are asleep, at least in theory. We'll look at the dilemma faced by people who've been managers for years and now are considering individual contributor roles, but are finding that their skills are out of date. Finally, we'll look at the new requirements employers are mandating whether in the form of new technical skills or the increasing desire for job candidates with certifications.

Managing Virtual Teams In The Global Workplace

Managing virtual teams, whether they report to you or not, is a key challenge of today's global workplace.

A virtual team can be a *manager with direct reports located all over the world* or with reports in different parts of his or her country.

In the next two cases, the team members don't report directly to the team leader.

Another kind of virtual team could be a *global training team.* This is often used for sales or technical sales people worldwide who need to be trained on new products and new skills on an ongoing basis. The team leader may be a training manager whose goal is to make sure each team member is trained effectively and can perform at a high level.

A *global product team* is another kind of virtual team where the project manager or product manager leads a team of people all over the world in different functional areas who need to collaborate to develop and deliver a new product. Here's a detailed look at how global teams work and the key skills required.

Members of global product teams are acutely aware of the realities of the global workplace. They attend meetings at all hours of the day and night. They work closely with colleagues in other countries who speak different native languages and have different cultural influences, levels of education, and work experience. Ideally, they need to function as though the entire team were co-located and able to talk to each other daily. Thanks to email, phone, and videoconferencing of documents, schedules, and specifications, marketing literature can be shared and edited collaboratively.

However, even though the technology is available to support optimal collaboration over long distances, people are still human. A number of my clients have ranted on numerous occasions about the needless complexities imposed on their work lives by being a part of global product teams. Each of the clients who felt frustrated with working in global product teams worked for a different company, but the rants were pretty similar.

A software engineer: "Even though we have the latest technology, we're still much more inefficient in a global product development team, because we can't talk freely with our overseas colleagues. I get much more information from a face-to-face technical conversation than through email, because for the most part, in an email dialogue, much that would be said casually face to face never gets said."

A business intelligence analyst: "Some of my overseas colleagues are very junior. Since they're inexperienced, they often make mistakes because they lack the judgment and experience of their senior colleagues. Then, they try to save face, and it takes a lot longer to solve the problem because they're unwilling to honestly share what's going on. I can usually solve the same problem in much less time. Even though I cost my employer more by the hour than these colleagues, by the time they've made the mistake, attempted to fix it a few times, then given up and asked for help, the whole problem ends up costing our project in days and therefore, in dollars.

A customer service engineer: "My company was acquired by a major multinational Enterprise software company, and now my workdays are much longer than they ever used to be. I'm a part of several global product teams. Every day I have early morning conference calls and/or late night conference calls. I feel like much of what's said on those calls isn't worth my time, but my manager insists I attend each call and checks the meeting summaries to make sure I attended."

A technical writer: "Some of my overseas colleagues don't understand, speak, or write English very well. This makes my job more challenging. The specifications I receive are often incorrect, which means I can't assume that the core information I'm working with is accurate. I end up spending extra time verifying data which should have been correct when it was sent to me. This costs our project days' worth of time."

Key Skills

Communication – It's quite clear that the number one skill in this global workplace is excellent written and verbal communication. Not everyone on your team may be a native English speaker, and if others' attempts at English frustrate you, take a moment to imagine what it would be like for you to do your work in their language.

Overcommunication is essential when dealing with others located remotely. Compensate for distance between you and your team members by being available to them via email or private phone conversation if necessary. Communicate what you want your team to know, check that they really understand what you want and when you want it, and then check back to make sure you'll get what you want when you want it. Be sure that non-native English speakers truly understand. Sometimes native English speakers don't understand what you said or what you want. Sometimes they're too embarrassed to admit they had no clue what you meant even if they understood your English. Make it easy for all team members to clarify information.

Interpersonal Skills and Teamwork – Be sure to develop good working relationships with everyone on your virtual team. Recognize the value each person adds to the team. This allows you to more easily solve problems, mitigate conflicts, and coach others who may need assistance.

Multicultural Awareness – Because the people on a global team come from different lands and cultures, it's crucial that each team member be aware of, and comfortable with cultural differences. Whether it's an accent that's hard to understand or a different approach to solving a problem, team members need to be able to learn to work with the differences. Be sure you understand the values of the other cultures you deal with so you don't inadvertently offend a team member.

Problem Solving – In global teams, it's wise to anticipate potential problems and create processes that support the overall goals and schedule the various team members are working toward. When unanticipated problems surface, be sure to come up with timely solutions so the whole team is not impacted or delayed by a problem in one area. The old saw "a chain is only as strong as its weakest link" applies to global teams too. If one group or team member is the "weak link," keep an eye on their progress, and be prepared to help them stay on track.

Flexibility – Because decisions are often made and changed in real time in today's global workplace, flexibility is essential. You can't be resistant to change. New rules, new schedules, new ways of working together, and new approaches are commonplace. You have to adapt quickly.

Technical Literacy – Basic computer, web, and Internet literacy is essential to the effective functioning of a global team. The underlying technology helps to provide the foundation for fast communication across time zones.

From Manager to Individual Contributor

My client Cliff has been a manager for over 10 years in both large and smaller technology companies. He's got a solid track record as a manager of hardware development teams. Even though he's great at getting products developed, tested, and shipped to customers, his most recent company folded, leaving him without a job. Despite his good network, Cliff has discovered there aren't many development manager jobs available these days. He decided he'd like to apply for individual contributor jobs as well.

As he analyzed the job postings and ads, he realized his technical skills were way out of date. Even though the people who worked for him had learned the newer skills and tools, he hadn't taken the time to update his technical ability.

Key Skills

Technical Skills – Determine which of the new up-to-date tools, techniques, and methods will have the biggest return on investment for your study time. What's worth taking the time to learn can be your hardest decision. Do some research before spending time and money to learn new skills. Are there any retraining programs you can join that will teach you these or similar valuable skills? Can you get temporary or contract jobs where you could learn some of them on the job?

Flexibility – Be willing to play a different role, dive into the details, and directly drive the results.

Teamwork – This will be a different experience as an individual contributor. Sometimes it's hard to resist the urge to lead when you're used to being the leader. Recognize the talents and strengths of the other members of your team and value each person. Beware of being a know-it-all and challenging your manager's authority. Remember that he or she may be concerned that you'll be a management nightmare.

New Technical Skills in Practice

My client Greg is an experienced software engineer who from time to time in his career also managed software teams or organizations. Even though he's a good manager, like most engineers, he really prefers to work in an engineering role solving technical problems rather than managing people or projects. He's worked for a series of successful startups and enjoys working in up-and-coming companies.

In the years following the Internet bubble, Greg chose to stay at the company he was working for rather than look for a more challenging job elsewhere. He was bored working in a dead end job, but during the recession, interesting jobs were few and far between. No one was getting raises at his company, and he wasn't looking for a promotion. He asked his boss for some assignments that would allow him to develop some new technical skills, but his boss was short staffed and couldn't afford to divert him to a non-critical project.

Greg finally got to the point where he was ready to look for a new job. He went about the task as he always had: contacted the people in his network, pursued interesting job options, and interviewed at a number of companies. Unlike every other time he'd looked for a job, this time he got no offers.

Working with me, Greg did an in-depth "Professional Competitiveness Checkup," and we discovered his technical skills were out of date. Even though he'd taken classes and learned the key new skills, *he'd never used them on the job*. Greg changed his strategy. He focused his job search on companies in technology areas he'd already worked in. Because he had the technical expertise and experience these companies valued, they seemed more willing to hire him. However, it took him another 12 months to get a solid job offer. He finally found a suitable job where he'd be using the key new skills he'd learned every day.

Key Skills

Technical Skills –In this particular case, Greg had taken classes and was an experienced software developer. He was trying to move into an area of software quite different from what he'd done before. Nowadays, it makes sense to offer your services to community groups or non-profits to create a real working system with your new skills so you can effectively showcase them to a prospective employer.

When making shifts from one type of software to another, it helps to make more gradual shifts so you can use something you've done before as a stepping stone to what you want to be doing that's new.

Problem Solving – Some hiring managers who are willing to give you the benefit of the doubt in the case where you've learned the skill but haven't used it on the job, will do a rigorous job of testing your problem-solving skills. Be prepared! But be aware that not all hiring managers will offer this leeway. I've noticed that the cases where hiring managers give you the benefit of the doubt is usually when you come highly recommended by someone they know and respect.

Interpersonal Skills – If you're in a situation like Greg's where he was a senior software professional interviewing with a group of much younger engineers, it's crucial to be able to create rapport and professional respect with the manager and the other engineers in the group. The younger engineers know you cost more than they do. If they don't perceive any advantage to hiring you (given what you cost) and/or they don't like you, even if the boss is sold on you, he won't hire you because he'll be concerned about how well you'll fit in. It's much easier for him to take a risk on a younger, less experienced engineer who has the exact skills he wants.

P.S. What's In It For My Career?

These days, hiring managers want job candidates to have done the exact same job they are offering beforehand at a previous company. Philosophically, I totally disagree with this way of thinking. Why would an intelligent person want to do the exact same job they've been doing at a previous company in a new environment? Some may say that because it's in a new environment, there'll be plenty to learn in the new company. Honestly, I wouldn't want to do the exact same job at a new company. Most intelligent people want to learn new skills, and if there isn't an element of something new I can learn in a new job, why would I want the job, even if the salary were better? As a job candidate who wants to stay in the driver's seat of my professional life, I would ask, "What's in it for my career?" I encourage you to do the same, by the way. Don't just take a job to do the same old things you know how to do—make sure you can learn something new!

From the manager's point of view, I can understand that a company might not want to spend time and resources training someone new, and they want to keep the learning curve short, but what about the candidate's need to grow their skill sets? I believe that job candidates are creative and resourceful and deserve to be thought of as such.

Hiring managers: Please be more open minded, see the possibilities in each person you interview, and look beyond their résumé to the real skills they'll offer your group.

Certifications – Are They Worth It?

A certification is an impartial, third-party endorsement of an individual's professional knowledge and experience. In order to get certified, a person has to take some classes and/or read some books, then take an exam. Since most business professions don't require licensure, and levels of education among corporate professionals vary, certifications are provided as a measure of the person's skill, ability, and knowledge in a specific discipline. Most certification programs are created, sponsored, or affiliated with professional or trade organizations interested in raising standards.

Certifications usually must be renewed periodically or may be valid for a specific period of time (e.g., the lifetime of the product for which the individual is certified). As a part of the renewal of a person's certification, the individual usually must show evidence of having attended continuing education classes or having earned continuing education units (CEUs).

The growth of certification programs is a reaction to the changing employment market. Certifications are portable, since they don't depend on one company's definition of a certain job. Nowadays, my clients in certain disciplines are telling me that employers are "requiring" certifications rather than making them "nice to have." By doing this, they're attempting to raise the bar on the quality of the applicants they're willing to look at and screening out the applicants who don't have the certifications. If you're otherwise qualified, make sure you don't get screened out just because you don't have a certification.

If you're in a profession where the lack of a certification is limiting the number of jobs you can apply for, you may want to consider getting certified. If you're not sure about this, ask around (i.e. recruiters, outplacement counselors, colleagues).

There are three general types of certification. Listed in order of development level and portability, they are: corporate (internal), product-specific, and profession-wide.

Corporate certifications are created by a corporation for internal purposes. For example, a corporation might require a one-day training course for all sales personnel, after which they receive a certificate. While this certificate has limited portability—to other corporations, for example—it's also the simplest to develop.

Product-specific certifications are more involved. They usually test product knowledge across all applications. This approach is prevalent in the information technology (IT) industry, where personnel are certified on a version of software or hardware. This type of certification is portable across locations (for example, different corporations that use that product), but not across other products.

Profession-wide certifications are the most general. In order to apply professional standards, increase the level of practice, and possibly protect the public, a professional organization might establish a certification. It's intended to be portable to all places a certified person might work. Because such programs are more general, they can be more costly. The process to establish a legally defensible assessment of an entire profession is quite extensive. An example would be a certified public accountant, who would not be certified for just one corporation or one piece of accounting software, but for general work in the profession. [23]

In addition to accounting, other business disciplines which now have certifications available include finance, project management, security, and IT.

Key Skills

Technical Skills – This is the information that's tested on the certification exam. If there's a course to prepare you for the exam, or a review course that highlights what you should be studying, take the course or find out from someone who has, exactly what material is covered on the exam. Be sure to spend your study time working on the right material. Take the time to read any books you might need to read.

Studying/Test Taking Skills – If it's been a while since you were in school, you may be out of practice at studying and test taking. If your memory isn't what it used to be, investigate what you can do to improve it. Once you know what to study, set up a study schedule so you can systematically prepare for the exam. If you prefer to study in a group, find others who are preparing for the exam and set up a study group. If working with a tutor would work best for you, do it. Don't waste time taking the test multiple times if you can avoid it. Take plenty of practice tests during your studying so you get a sense of how well prepared you are and what topics need more attention.

Planning and Follow Through – Not only do you need to study the material and take practice tests, but it's easier to prepare for an exam if you have a test date in mind. If the test is only offered a few times a year on specified dates, it'll be a lot easier to create a plan for yourself. But if the test is available any time you want to take it, having a specific date in mind and a study plan makes it a lot easier to avoid procrastination.

Two Levels of Skills

Regardless of what your job title is, certain job skills are expected in most industries. Since the beginning of your career, you've learned many new skills on the job and may also have taken various classes or trainings to learn other skills.

When it comes to job skills, there are two levels:

1. *Baseline skills*
   What every person who does what you do, needs to know to do their job.

For example, if you are a software engineer, baseline skills would be languages, source code control systems, writing specifications, and promoting the efficiency of the code.

What are your baseline skills?

2. *Specialty skills*

   Specialty skills often involve understanding the needs of a particular market or set of customers.

   Specialty skills for a software engineer might include:
   - How to develop software products for the design automation market.
   - How to write Enterprise software.
   - How to build web applications.

   In addition to specific market or customer knowledge, there may be specific tools or techniques required in your area of specialty.
   - What are they?
   - How good are you at using them?
   - What are your specialty skills?

Here's Where You Can Find Out What Skills Employers Are Looking For:

Ask:
- Your colleagues
- Recruiters
- Outplacement services
- Professional conferences
- Your professional organization

Check:
- Job postings
- Job sites like Monster.com
- Online groups: Yahoo groups, Google groups, LinkedIn groups
- Professional publications: industry magazines or your profession's journal

Don't wait until you're looking for a job to find out what skills employers are paying top dollar for! Stay in touch with the skills the market values, and be sure you learn them.

Exercise

1. *Write* an ad for your next job, (the next job you want) being specific about what skills are required.

2. *Research* - After you've written the ad, check current listings to find out what skills employers are looking for, for a similar job.

3. *Compare* to see how close your ad is to what's being advertised for.

4. *Determine* what you can do to get the skills you need.

Questions for you to ponder

Ask yourself these questions to test your awareness; not realizing you're "out of date" could bite you when you least expect it.

- *How up to date are your skills?*
- What job skills are required these days for someone in your area of expertise?
- What baseline or specialty skills are employers looking for today that you don't have?
- Do you have the skills that employers are willing to pay top dollar for?
- How do you keep up with the skills the market is paying top dollar for?
- How often do you actively upgrade your job skills?

Here are Some Ways to Update Your Business and Technical Skills:

Classes

Whether they're offered live in your community, at your place of employment, via teleclasses, online as distance learning or webinars, with others or privately, it helps to take advantage of the many classes available where you can learn new skills. Check out the offerings from:

Continuing Education – These courses or workshops may be offered by vendors who serve your profession and can include university extension courses or adult education. They vary in price, and the quality depends on who's teaching them. Do some research to find out how new and up to date the material is before taking the class.

Community Colleges – Whether you choose weekend workshops, evening classes, or online classes, the variety of educational opportunities available to working professionals at a good price is impressive. The price is usually terrific, and again the quality depends on the teacher. Check out the classes to see how new and up to date the content is before signing up.

Professional Associations you belong to may sponsor classes or lectures of interest to their members. Some of these are free to members and others may require a nominal fee.

Online Webinars – More and more of these online classes are now available from a variety of sources including vendors mentioned here. A webinar lets the student view an interactive computer screen for a visual as well as auditory learning experience.

Teleclasses or Teleseminar Series – These are highly effective for busy professionals. Often they're recorded and available for download if you can't attend live. Teleclasses are offered on just about any subject you can imagine.

Distance Learning or Self-Study Programs – Great for people who enjoy learning outside a class setting and are motivated enough to complete them. Unless you're sure you love learning by reading and find the interaction with an instructor a waste of time, try one distance learning course to be certain you enjoy this process before signing up for a complete distance learning program.

Personal or Group Coaching – Helpful for getting you unstuck with respect to a problem or problems you specify, such as implementing the strategies in this book. Group coaching is generally less expensive than personal coaching, and you get the benefit of others' questions and experiences. If you prefer to have all the attention on your questions and challenges and a one-to-one dialogue, then choose personal coaching. If I can be of help to you as a coach or mentor write to me nina@ninaprice. com.

Mentoring – The difference between mentoring and coaching is subtle. Mentors are more likely to give you specific advice based on their own experience and expertise, while coaches are more likely to ask insight-producing questions allowing you to derive your own answers. Mentoring is sometimes more expensive than coaching.

Your employer may offer professional development classes, lunchtime talks, or lectures. And they may offer compensation for you to update your skills, covering the cost of the classes and your other possible expenses.

Tackle Projects Where You Use the New Skills

Once you've learned the new skills, use them to do something valuable. This will deepen your knowledge and possibly give you a sample to show others how skillful you are.

On the job – Persuade your boss to let you use your new skills to do a project that never seems to climb to the top of the priority list. (Be sure not to neglect your other work that has a higher priority.)

Help a non-profit organization by using your skills to solve a problem for them. You can help an organization you believe in, and they'll get the benefit of having a problem solved.

You can even teach a class on how to do something useful with what *you've learned or teach others how to do the specific skill you learned.*

What can you do in the next 90 days to improve your skills and make yourself more irresistible to prospective employers?

Here's Your Challenge:

Whether you're **between jobs and feeling precarious**, **underemployed** (with or without golden handcuffs), or **hanging on to your job by your fingernails**, what's the first thing you can do to update your job skills that will have the highest payback during the next month? How could you take that step? Please take that step now!

Chapter

13

Professional Competitiveness Defined

Pulling All 5 Strategies Together and Implementing Them

The difference between great people and everyone else is that great people create their lives actively, while everyone else is created by their lives, passively waiting to see where life takes them next. The difference between the two is the difference between living fully and just existing.

~ Michael Gerber

Professional Competitiveness is about actively creating the professional life you *really* want.

There's nothing passive about it.

Creating the professional life you want is a process of constantly understanding and improving your value in the marketplace, while at the same time taking incredibly good care of yourself, so you can be resilient to the stresses and strains of a work environment defined by constant change.

Here's what Professional Competitiveness looks like:

- Staying employed and growing professionally no matter what happens in the economy, in your industry, in your company, or in your workgroup.

- Staying attractive to your current employer and other potential employers.

- Having the professional opportunities you want (jobs, promotions, raises, stock options, assignments).

- Working for as long as you want and retiring when you choose to, on your timetable.

> *Never continue in a job you don't enjoy. If you're happy*
> *in what you're doing, you'll like yourself, you'll have*
> *inner peace. And if you have that, along with physical*
> *health, you will have had more success than you could*
> *possibly have imagined.*
>
> ~ Johnny Carson

The Components of Professional Competitiveness are:

- **Stress Management:** Understanding what causes your stress and knowing how you can best respond to stressors is the key to resilience.

- **Health and Wellness:** Since you're the author of your own level of health and wellness or disease and illness, learn how to be fully in charge of your health. Enlist the assistance of others who can assist you if and when you need it.

- **Showcase Your Value:** The intelligence, motivation, skills, know how, ingenuity, and hard work you apply to your best contributions form the core of the value you add to your company. The value you contribute should always be obvious to your management, your peers, your colleagues, and your customers.

- **Manage Others' Perceptions of You:** Like it or not, first and lasting impressions count, especially in your professional life.

- Be sure you understand how others perceive you, and actively address or defy any stereotypes or distractions that could be undermining others' perceptions of you.

- **Interpersonal Skills:** Communicating your ideas, your knowledge, and your value through written words and conversation is crucial to your effectiveness in any professional situation, as is knowing how to negotiate for what you need.

- **Business Savvy:** The more you understand how the organization where you're currently employed *really* works, the more you'll become a key player, a uniquely valuable employee who's hard to replace.

- **Your Professional Network:** Who you know can be an extremely valuable asset in all aspects of your professional life, not just when you're looking for a job. Cultivate your network, especially when you don't need to rely on it.

- **Business/Technical Skills:** These skills are most likely the reason you were hired in the first place, but if you haven't kept them up to date, others who may cost your employer less may in fact be better qualified to do what you do.

Taking Action to Implement the 5 Strategies

"Making Lemonade" out of a challenging situation works best when you're honest with yourself about what needs to change. The next step is being willing to make the changes.

When it seems everything is "working," we avoid making changes even though we know it could be working better. Hopefully, by this point you've noticed what you need to change.

Are you ready and willing to make the changes?

Do you see what you're missing out on by not changing?

What could help you become more willing to make changes and to actually make those changes?

The Story of the Crow and the Pitcher

A crow perishing with thirst saw a pitcher, and hoping to find water, flew to it with delight. When he reached it, he discovered that it contained so little water he couldn't possibly get at it. He tried everything he could think of to reach the water, but all his efforts were in vain. At last, he collected as many stones as he could carry and dropped them one by one with his beak into the pitcher, until he brought the water within his reach and thus saved his life.

Moral: Necessity is the mother of invention.

Seven Steps to Professional Competitiveness

Here's a process you can use to take action on each of the 5 strategies. Since necessity is the mother of invention, use this process as a starting point and modify the steps to suit your specific situation.

1. *Take a Good Look at Yourself and Your Life* with respect to each of the 5 strategies.
   - What are your biggest health challenges?
   - What else can you do to be in the best health possible?
   - What are the biggest sources of stress in your life right now?
   - How is stress showing up in your body (sleeping problems, headaches, low back pain, etc.)?
   - Do you have a chronic illness?
   - If so, how is stress affecting your illness?
   - When was the last time you got a raise or a promotion?
   - When was the last time your boss acknowledged your contribution to the company?
   - Do you have a personal brand? If so, what is it?
   - What is your expertise?
   - Who in your company knows you're an expert?
   - How do you showcase your expertise?
   - How could you make a better first impression?

- Which of the stereotypes about older workers apply to you?
- How could you present yourself more effectively?
- Do you cultivate a network of colleagues and friends who can offer you helpful information and connections?
- Do you pay attention to your network on a regular basis?
- Do you stay in touch with the people in your network when you're not looking for a job?
- Are you involved in social networking? How can you use it to benefit your career?
- How up to date or out of date are your job skills?
- What job skills could you cultivate that employers are willing to pay top dollar for?

2. *Figure Out What's Working and What's Not* in each of the five areas. Be completely honest with yourself. What's not working any more for you?

3. *Decide What Needs to Change and Prioritize the Changes* – You'll most likely discover that you already know what needs to change but haven't yet implemented the changes you most need to make. Don't be complacent! Be proactive!

4. *Develop a Blueprint and Determine How You Will be Accountable* – Remember to set up what you need to hold yourself accountable. Is it some concrete deadlines? Do you need a partner or buddy to work with? How about a mentor or coach? How will you make sure you get started and actually finish each step?

5. *Work Your Plan and Track Your Progress* – See where you are in 30, 60, and 90 days. Be honest with yourself: what's working and what's not working? What can help you succeed with what's not working?

6. *Get Help If You Need Help* – Hiring a good coach or mentor can be the best self-care money you'll spend this year. If you need help with a health issue, get assistance soon; don't put it off.

7. *Celebrate Your Successes and Share Your Success Stories* – Please write and tell me about what you've accomplished at nina@ninaprice.com. I'd love to hear about your successes and your experiences along the way. I promise to congratulate you.

Learn More

The 5 strategies we've looked at here are extremely important, but implementing them is only the beginning of your journey to professional competitiveness.

If you need help, consider getting some coaching or mentoring either in a group or individually. The SHARPEN YOUR COMPETITIVE EDGE programs offer several options. Check out my website for details at www.ninaprice.com/prevent-burnout.html.

One of the programs is a weekend workshop, SHARPEN YOUR COMPETITIVE EDGE: How to Stay Professionally Competitive in a Rapidly Changing World, in which you get an in-depth Professional Competitiveness Checkup and leave with a blueprint and coaching program to support you in turning your blueprint into reality. www.sharpenyourcompetitiveedge.info

Just by reading this book, you're taking the first step to pushing the reset button on your career. If you've actively sought answers to some of the questions asked here, you're beyond the first step. Now take the next step!

Take incredibly good care of yourself and your professional life, so you'll be prepared to enjoy the rest of your life.

Chapter

14

Professional Competitiveness: What Success Looks Like

Being in the Driver's Seat

Hank contacted me out of the blue after receiving my latest newsletter. He lives in another part of the U.S. from where I live, and he phoned me to catch up after about five years. He and his wife are in the enviable position of being able to take the summer off to spend time with their children who are 10 and 12. Hank's wife recently sold her company for a substantial amount and is thinking about what she wants to do next; Hank himself is between jobs. They're considering relocating to another part of the U.S. Like most people between jobs, Hank is looking for a new gig that's interesting to him. He's not ready to retire, or play golf all day, or just coach his kids' sports teams. He's been considered for a series of jobs but hasn't found the right fit, yet.

As he caught me up on the last few years, I learned that he'd had a job involving quite a bit of travel to another state. He'd done some real estate investing in the state he'd been working in and had profitably flipped a number of houses while the market was good. He'd kept his eye on the ball financially and was now glad he had.

Hank has been taking care of himself and his career. He stays fit, watches his weight, takes care of his health, and is careful not to become complacent. His skills are solid, and he stays in touch with people in his network. Even though he's between jobs, right now he can afford to take some time off. Hank's in the driver's seat in his life. I pointed that out to him, and I could see him smiling, even though he was in a different time zone and we were talking by phone.

He was interested in the thoughts I've shared in this book, and I asked him what advice he had for my readers.

Hank's advice:

- Keep your costs in check! The people he sees struggling the most have a high monthly burn rate: houses, boats, fancy cars, child support, alimony, maxed out credit cards, and more.

- Invest the money you have wisely, and just like your career, keep your eye on your investments.

- Create passive income so you have revenue even when you don't have a job.

Hank is really clear that he's not planning to rely on a corporate job as his sole source of income, or as he says in the vernacular, "I'm not going to be a bitch to any corporation ever again!"

Hank has kept his costs down, and he's diversified his investments. Creating passive income was important to him and it paid off. Passive income makes a lot of sense for all families. If you haven't already, investigate passive income possibilities you would be interested in. Hank invested in real estate and did some options trading. Others I talked to created information products or participated in multilevel marketing. A simple way to become convinced of the power of passive income is to play Robert Kiyosaki's *Cashflow 101* board game.

Offer Your Employer Value in Trade for an Opportunity to Do Something New

I hadn't seen Francisco for about a year when he texted me requesting an acupuncture appointment the next day. Fortunately, I had an appointment available that suited his schedule. South American born, he's tall, dashing, and always impeccably groomed. "No one can put me back together as well as you can," he said. I felt honored by his trust in me.

He's doing a different job than the last time we spoke. I asked him how he's stayed employed in this economy. "I'm really clear about the value I'm offering my employer," he said. "I always look for a new job where I can expand my skills. I get to try something new while offering my employer what I already know that I'm good at. A job where I'm not learning anything new doesn't work for me. Some months ago, my current employer had a small layoff, but they decided to keep me because I have skills that no one else on their staff has, and they know they need my skills."

Francisco did a great job of positioning himself with his new employer. They hired him because he had skills they needed that no one else had. They kept him on staff because of those same skills. He wanted to get more sales experience, and this job allows him to do some sales, so he's growing his skill set while offering his employer something valuable— his other skills.

Deliver Consistent Value and Ask For What You Want

My client Emily was so excited she almost couldn't speak coherently. She called me in the middle of the afternoon the other day because she couldn't wait to share her news. Recently she'd felt frustrated because she was aware that others in her organization had been promoted. Even though the financials at her company had been lackluster of late, her general manager wanted to retain key managers that she valued. Emily hadn't been notified of a promotion, although she felt strongly that her performance and the key strategic work she'd been doing for her general manager merited a promotion. We discussed the pros and cons of asking for a promotion and came up with a strategy she felt confident about.

That day Emily had had lunch with her general manager and asked her what her development plan was for Emily. The general manager surprised Emily by acknowledging the value of Emily's work and by offering her both a promotion and a raise! Emily was thrilled. She knew her boss valued her work, which had been consistently of high quality. Her boss also values Emily's loyalty and acknowledged that Emily always goes the extra mile in everything she does at work.

Emily asked for what she wanted and got it. Even though her results were outstanding, she felt some trepidation about asking for a promotion. She didn't want to "back her boss into a corner" and risk tarnishing their relationship. She figured out how to make it easy for her boss to offer her a promotion, and her boss kindly offered the raise, which Emily wasn't expecting.

A year ago, I might have described Emily's situations as "underemployed." Her previous general manager didn't understand her value at all.

Your Success Story Belongs Here:

Write and share your success story. Use the 5 Strategies Facebook page to share your successes and inspire others.

http://tinyurl.com/http-facebook5strategies

Chapter

15

Bonus Chapter:
Social Networking – A Tutorial

Focused on LinkedIn and Facebook, with some additional thoughts about Blogging

Even though there are now many excellent social networking sites available, the two most useful ones for business people are LinkedIn and Facebook. If you're new to social networking, I suggest you start with these two, and then investigate others if you're so inclined.

Your Social Networking Profile – Another First Impression

Each social networking site asks you to create a profile when you join. Your profile page is yet another important first impression you make. Your online profile is like a résumé, business card, and your personal brand all in one place. Be sure to create a profile consistent with your personal brand.

On LinkedIn, and sometimes on Facebook, potential employers, hiring managers, and recruiters may be taking a look at you via your profile. Your job is to give them an overview of who you are, what you've done, and why they should be interested in you. You can also call attention to yourself by posting comments and participating in discussions. Your profile is about affirming your credibility.

Since your profile is so important to your credibility, here are some suggestions based on insights from two social networking experts, Nancy Marmolejo of www.VivaVisibility.com and Mari Smith of www. MariSmith.com, about how to create a social networking profile that will make a great first impression. [24]

Check Out Others' Profiles – Determine what you'll emulate and what you'll avoid. Since imitation is the sincerest form of flattery, see what you find appealing and attractive in other people's profiles, and decide how you'll emulate that. If there are aspects of their profile you find distracting or unattractive, be sure you don't do the same things.

Lead With Your Expertise and Confidence – An attractive profile leads with your expertise and has a confident tone. It clearly states who you are, what you do, and the results you help create. Don't make people dig too deeply into your copy to find out who you are and how they can benefit from hiring you.

Add Some Relevant Personal Information – Once your professional expertise is clear, it's okay to add a bit of interesting personal information. Include what you feel most comfortable with, such as hobbies, sports, achievements, or fun quirky things you think others might find appealing. Use judgment here, so you don't undermine the credibility you've established.

Be Sure to Include a Great Photo – Choose a photo that shows your face clearly, not a distant photo of you in a big crowd. Experts say a picture of you looking directly at the camera will create a connection faster with your viewer than pictures of you looking away from the camera. Be honest with your profile picture, using a fairly recent photo, not one from 10 or more years ago.

Make it Easy for People to Learn More About You – Make certain you include links to your website, your blog, and other social networking sites you participate in, if you want to share that information. Be sure all your links are "live" by using http:// in each web address.

Give Your Profile the 10-Second Test – You have no more than 10 seconds to make an impression on visitors who come to your social networking profile pages. Some experts say you have even less time than that, so make sure it's easy to get who you are, what you do, and what your results are. Be sure to double check your formatting, and make certain all the paragraphs aren't lumped into one big block of text.

Get Some Feedback on Your Profile – Ask friends and people who know you to take a look at your profile and give you feedback before a recruiter does. Just like your résumé, you want to be confident your social networking profile represents you in the best possible way.

Now that you've built your social networking profile:

- Be clear about what you want to accomplish with social networking – Develop a strategy and a plan to achieve your goals. Are you looking for a job? Interested in meeting people in your profession? Or who went to the same graduate school that you did? Do you want to reconnect with people who worked at a company you did?

- Participate in the social networking communities you've joined and become an active member – Be consistent with your strategy. Stay visible and involved.

- Give others feedback – Whether it's commenting on their blog posts or noticing something effective they've done to their profile page, being positive and generous builds positive connections.

- Be helpful when you can – Answer questions and offer referrals or resources. Hopefully, others will help to promote what you're up to when you need them to. People feel compelled to reciprocate your kindness, so give first, and see great responses.

- Connect your content to your social networking profiles – You can have your blog posts and articles appear on your profile page; it's yet another place people interested in you can read them.

- Write recommendations for people you think well of – LinkedIn allows you to recommend people you may have worked with or whose work you know about. This allows other people to read what you have to say about potential connections, possible employees, or prospective clients. And when you have other people recommending you, you can point potential clients or employers to those recommendations so they're more confident in your abilities.

- Update your profile and your status regularly – Let your network stay current and aware of what you're up to and what's new in your world.

LINKEDIN

http://www.linkedin.com

LinkedIn is great for business and professional people. Creating a profile there positions you as both a business person and a professional.

I encourage all my coaching clients who are looking for a job to reconnect on LinkedIn with every colleague they've ever enjoyed working with. It's a great way to catch up and reconnect with people you're out of touch with. Through reconnecting on LinkedIn, my clients have gotten job leads, and they've gotten clues about who's hiring and what skills they're paying the most for.

Ask people you've worked with to endorse you by writing a recommendation of your work. This can be especially valuable when your recommender is someone your connections or prospective employers know and respect.

Consider joining groups set up for people who have common interests, who went to your school, who worked for the same company as you, or who do what you do. You can join up to 50 groups. When you join a group, introduce yourself so others know who you are. You can even provide links to your profile, your website, and your blog. Be polite and thank people who answer your questions; make constructive comments, and be helpful to others in the group.

Encourage others to visit your profile and link to you by including the URL of your profile in your email signature.

Remember that your LinkedIn profile can be more easily found by search engines if you include plenty of searchable keywords in your profile and your posts.

FACEBOOK

http://www.facebook.com

- Facebook offers some valuable features not available at LinkedIn:

- Facebook is simpler to use than LinkedIn. It's easier to "friend" people on Facebook, because you're not required to know their email addresses.

- On Facebook people are having conversations and sharing what they're doing. You can create a private group where you can share and discuss information relevant to that group.

- Facebook feeds offer you a constant stream of information that you are specifically interested in. You can choose to read the latest international news, what your friends and associates are up to, or the latest posts from blogs you follow. Feeds can also come from Flickr, Digg, YouTube, Yelp, del.icio.us, Google Reader, and other services.

- Facebook offers more third party applications. These are definitely worth checking out!

- You can link Facebook to your blog, to Twitter, and to other applications.

- Both Facebook and LinkedIn are useful tools when looking for a job, researching a company, participating in groups, finding information, and reconnecting with people you've worked with.

If you'd like to learn more about ins and outs of Facebook, check out Mari Smith's blog: http://whyfacebook.com.

Regardless of which social networking platforms you use, it's wise to have a strategy for how you will use them. Here are a few suggestions:

1. Have definite criteria for who you want in your network – Do you want people you've worked with in the past? People you currently work with? People you admire? People you've met but would like to know better? People who can recommend you?

2. Focus on relationship building – Once people are in your network, stay in touch with them by:

    • Posting updates so people know what you're doing.

    • Commenting on their updates, photos, videos, and notes. I was amazed at how many people wished me a "Happy Birthday" because of Facebook. I have to admit it felt great.

    • If someone you know is hosting an event that is open to the public or doing something else of interest, share information about it with people you think would be interested to support the host and to create viral visibility.

3. Be deliberate about what you do with social networking – Others will notice what you endorse, so make sure you endorse people and things you support and believe in.

    Things to beware of:

    • Growing your network too quickly. On Facebook you can have your account deactivated if you grow your network too quickly. Take your time to build up a strategic network of friends focusing on quality, not quantity. Your social circle will grow naturally over time anyway. You can only be friends with 5,000 people on Facebook, so pick them carefully.

    • It's wise not to send more than 20 new friend requests at any one time.

    • "Romeos" are people who are flirting and are clearly not looking for business contacts.

When you contribute comments, be sure they add value. Commenting for the sake of commenting is like arguing for the sake of arguing—it makes you look less than attractive.

TWITTER

What I've found most rewarding about Twitter is the ability to engage in instant conversations. You can see how people are responding to the latest news, new ideas and trends. You can find out about helpful information you weren't aware of. You can meet people you might have no other way of meeting.

Twitter Terminology

Microblog – posting ideas and thoughts in 140 characters..

Tweet – up to 140 characters of commentary or information.

Retweet [RT] – share what someone else on Twitter has said being sure to attribute what they've said to them.

Following – people whose tweets you've decided to watch.

Tweetstream – what the people you're following are saying on Twitter.

Avatar – a photo of you that represents you as you want others to see you and think of you.

Direct Message [DM] – private 140 character message from you to someone else on Twitter.

Getting Yourself Set Up on Twitter

Your Twitter ID – ideally use your own name. This should be how you want people to think of you when they meet you.

Your Twitter Bio – you get 160 characters to share about yourself. You can use this to share your personal/professional brand.

The Look of your Twitter Page – You can use the backgrounds Twitter provides or you can "pimp your page". See what others have done and decide how to best reflect yourself and your brand on your Twitter page.

How to Tweet

Some Twitter experts say you should Tweet several times per day.

> **Focus on:**
> * Following people whose ideas you are interested in
> * Replying to direct messages people send you
> * Retweeting sharing helpful information that others have shared with you, and giving them credit for sharing it with you
> * Sharing helpful information on the topics you tweet about

What can I say in 140 characters?

Not much so it's important to pay attention to what you say – lots of people could be reading it.

What is Twitter good for?

- Meeting people and building relationships
- Learning about interesting and useful resources
- Finding out what others are doing
- Letting people know what you're doing (but not too much)

Building Credibility

- Establish Yourself as an Expert
- Be Knowledgeable
- Be honest and Reliable
- Be Likeable and Friendly
- Interact with Others

Make sure that your bio represents you well, your page looks good, your tweets make sense and that you're generally adding value.

Pick Your Topics – decide on a list of four or five topics that you'll tweet about, ideally ones that have to do with your expertise and your interests.

Decide on who you'll follow and who you won't. Have a set of decision rules about who you'll follow. Here's a sample set:

- People in my industry
- People in my profession
- People I would like to meet
- People I have met personally

If you are just getting started and are a bit uncertain how to go about building a following. Here are a few ideas:

- Start following people that you want to follow you - many of them will reciprocate. You can start by following me: http://www.twitter.com/ninapricelac

- Ask your colleagues and friends whether they are on Twitter. Add your Twitter address to your email signature or invite people to follow you on Twitter on your blog or website.

How can I use Twitter to make others aware of what I have to offer?

80-90% of your tweets should be about your topics and can include quotes, recipes, retweets, or pointers to useful info

10-20% of your tweets should be about what you're doing.

I look forward to reading your tweets.

Thoughts about Blogging

I've never been a person who kept a journal or diary, so it took me a while to embrace blogging. I've decided that blogging is great for people who have wonderful insights and ideas, as well as plenty of opinions. Blogging can help you build a community and showcase your expertise or insights.

But first you need to have something to say that other people want to read. Always write content that you think people will find interesting, enjoyable, or valuable. It helps if you teach, explain, or give directions on how to do something of interest to your readers. It also helps if your ideas are thought provoking. Be sure to take stands on issues you care about that are also important to your readers; controversy attracts readers.

Here are a few thoughts about blogging if you decide to start a blog:

WordPress is one of a number of popular blogging tools. Many people use it because you can create your own blog or even a web page for free. This is a terrific way to get started with minimum investment of time and money. If you love to do things yourself and have limited resources, but want a blog or web page, head for http://www.wordpress.com.

Before you create your own blog do some research.

- Look at 10-20 different blogs that your potential reader might be viewing.

- Whose blog(s) do you like?

- What do you like about these blogs?

- What will you emulate from these blogs in your blog?

How to get started with a blog:

- What will you write about? (topics)
- What will you call your blog?
- Do you want a memorable URL that reflects your blog's name or topics?
- Who do you want to read your blog?
- How will you make your ideal reader aware of your blog?

Your About Page explains who you are, what you're blogging about, and why someone would want to read your blog. Be clear about what's in it for them.

Your Contact Page should make it easy for your readers to get in touch with you, so include any contact details you choose. Also, post a quality photo of yourself to make your blog more personal. This is a good idea if you want to create a dialogue with your readers.

Pillar Articles are substantial articles that teach subjects relevant to your blog theme. Ideally these are original articles that demonstrate your expertise and insights. Pillar articles are blog posts that are effective at driving readers and backlinks (other sites linking to your blog) to your blog. A pillar article provides timeless information—it's relevant to a wide audience for a long period of time. It could provide a definition of a key term, answer a commonly asked question, or include a brief how-to tutorial. It may offer a reason to bookmark and/or subscribe to your blog (and RSS feed). Generally, these articles are longer than 500 words and have lots of practical information or advice. The more pillar articles you have on your blog the better, because they eventually bring in traffic from search engines (because so many other web pages link to them).

In contrast, a spike article is one that generates a quick rush of traffic to your blog that often disappears within a day or two and has very little long-lasting impact. Pillar articles are timeless, while spike articles are temporary.

Here are accomplished blogger Yaro Starak's thoughts about good topics for pillar articles:

1. The "How-To" Article

Think about your industry and write an article that teaches how to do something relevant to your area of expertise. Be certain to only write how-to articles on topics you genuinely understand and have experience with. Include a story if you can.

2. The Definition Article

Many industries have key concepts which new readers wouldn't be aware of. If a concept is complicated, write a pillar article that defines the concept, clearly explaining what it means and how it can be implemented.

These key concepts may seem simple and obvious to you, but remember you're an expert in your field, so explain it to the newbies in simple terms and, of course, try to tell a story as an example.

A glossary or definition page is a good pillar article. If there are a handful of key concepts in your industry, write an article that lists the concepts and provide a one-paragraph definition for each. A resource page like this is good as a reference piece and may often be referred back to by other bloggers and websites.

Describe each concept in your own words, using your own unique story and voice. This helps to build credibility and trust. It's always wiser to include your own version of a definition when you're capable of explaining a term or concept, rather than link to other sites and drive traffic away from your blog.

3. Present a Theory or Argument

Write an article discussing your theories or opinions about a key issue in your industry.

Be sure to present some unique thoughts. What's important is that you write about a topic you suspect your readers will take an interest in. Don't just rehash what other people have said and present your own thesis. Stimulate conversation or controversy about a topic that's often discussed and isn't time-dependent. This will draw traffic to your blog.

4. Create a Free Report or Whitepaper

A document like a whitepaper (a 2-10 page document, which teaches how to do something) or a series of articles combined to create a report, works well as a pillar. You can create a PDF file, which your readers can download.

The important thing with this concept is to create a complete all-in-one solution to a common problem. Similar to the how-to article, a free resource is a powerful pillar concept because it demonstrates your expertise and brings in consistent traffic.

5. A List Article

You've probably seen many of these at other blogs. The usual titles are "Top 7 Ways To…" or "10 Tips To Improve…" etc. These work well because:

1. Lists are easily digested. It's been tested and proven that articles in the 300-700 word range with lots of clear bulleted lists and a compelling headline are good traffic pullers. In this case, it's all about simplicity of consumption for people with short attention spans, i.e. most web surfers.

2. Lists provide directly actionable lessons, and people love to share lists with other people. Consequently, list articles are often linked to by other bloggers and added to social bookmarking sites that drive traffic.

Provided your list follows all the standard pillar concept rules—timeless, original content, problem-solving ideas—and you keep it directly applicable to your audience, most lists will become pillars.

Be wary of doing lists of topics well covered by other people or on really simple concepts. As usual, the more "you" included through stories and a unique style, the more likely your list will perform well.

6. A Technical Blueprint

A technical blueprint is very much like a how-to or a whitepaper, but is focused on the technical aspects of a problem. Technology-focused bloggers are good at writing blueprint pillar articles because they love to use graphs, spreadsheets, and images to demonstrate how to do something.

A technical blueprint is a step-by-step, visually enhanced article demonstrating exactly how to complete a task. Often the pictures tell the story more than the words do. Designers and programmers use this style of blog post to show how they code a website, design an image using Photoshop, code software, or perform simpler activities like attaching a file to an email.

You can apply the principle to almost any industry that has common tasks which may be complex to understand. In this case, it's more about the imagery and less about the story. [25]

You can read more of Yaro Starak's ideas at http://www.entrepreneurs-journey.com.

References

1.   The U.S. Equal Employment Opportunity Commission. Facts About Age Discrimination. Retrieved July 26, 2009 from the World Wide Web:

http://www.eeoc.gov/facts/age.html

2.   Haaga, John. (2002, December). "Just How Many Baby Boomers Are There?"

Population Reference Bureau. Retrieved July 26, 2009 from the World Wide Web: http://www.prb.org/Articles/2002/JustHowManyBabyBoomersAreThere.aspx

3.   U.S. Census Bureau. (2009, April). Unemployed persons by age, sex, and marital status. Retrieved July 26, 2009 from the World Wide Web: ftp://ftp.bls.gov/pub/suppl/empsit.cpseea9.txt

4.   Reeves, Scott. (2005, September 28). "An Aging Workforce's Effect on U.S. Employers." Forbes. Retrieved July 26, 2009 from the World Wide Web:

http://www.forbes.com/2005/09/28/career-babyboomer-workcx_sr_0929bizbasics.html

5.   Merrill Lynch. (2005, February 22). "The New Retirement Survey from Merrill Lynch

Shows How Baby Boomers Will Transform Retirement." Retrieved July 26, 2009 from the World Wide Web: http://www.agewave.com/media_files/pr3.pdf

6.   Ibid.

7.   Towers Perrin. (2006, October) The Aging Workforce: Challenge or Opportunity?

Retrieved July 26, 2009 from the World Wide Web:

http://www.towersperrin.com/tp/getwebcachedoc?webc=HRS/USA/2006/200610/aging_workforce.pdf

8.   AARP. "Staying Ahead of the Curve 2007 The AARP Work and Career Study."

Retrieved July 26, 2009 from the World Wide Web:

http://www.aarp.org/research/work/employment/work_career_08.html

9.   Merrill Lynch. Op Cit.

10.   Edington,Dee. "Emerging research — a view from one research center", American Journal of Health Promotion, 2001,volume 15:5, page 346.

11.   Rotstein, Gary. (2007, March 18) "Boomer Health Decline Reported." Pittsburgh Post

Gazette. Retrieved July 26, 2009 from the World Wide Web:

http://www.post-gazette.com/pg/07077/770461-114.stm

12.   Stein, Rob. (2007, April 20) "Baby Boomers Appear to Be Less Healthy Than Parents."

Washington Post. Retrieved July 26, 2009 from the World Wide Web:

http://www.washingtonpost.com/wpdyn/content/article/2007/04/19/AR2007041902458.html

13.   Mendoza, Allie. (2009, July). "Obesity epidemic 101: What are the obesity statistics in the United States?" San Francisco Examiner. Retrieved July 26, 2009 from the World Wide Web: http://www.examiner.com/x-15753-SF-Wellness-Examiner~y2009m7d26-Obesity-epidemic-101-What-are-the-obesity-statistics-in-the-United-States

14.   Wikipedia. (2009, May 24) "Baby Boom Generation." Retrieved July 26, 2009 from the World Wide Web: http://en.wikipedia.org/wiki/Baby_Boom_Generation

15.   Rotstein, Gary. Op Cit.

16.   AARP. Op Cit.

17.   AARP. (2008, June) "In Brief: How Is the Age Discrimination in Employment Act Working? A Look Back and Into the Future." Research Report.mk. Retrieved July 26, 2009 from the World Wide Web:

http://www.aarp.org/research/work/agediscrim/inb159_adea.html

18. Briand, Paul. (2009, March 12) "Baby Boomers Face Workplace Ageism." San Francisco Examiner. Retrieved July 26, 2009 from the World Wide Web:

http://www.examiner.com/x-654-Baby-Boomer-Examiner-~y2009m3d12-Baby-Boomers-Face-Workplace-ageism

19. Ibid.

20. Namli, Umit. "7 Health Benefits of Drinking Water" Sports and Cooking Your Blog for

 Healthy Living. Retrieved July 26, 2009 from the World Wide Web:

http://sportsandcooking.com/health/7-health-benefits-of-drinking-water

21. Goleman, Daniel. (1986, May 13) "Relaxation: Surprising Benefits Detected." New York

Times. Retrieved July 26, 2009 from the World Wide Web:

    http://www.nytimes.com/1986/05/13/science/relaxation-surprising-benefits- detected.html?sec=health

22. Allen, Debbie and Jeffrie Story. Confessions of Shameless Self Promoters. Retrieved July 26, 2009 from the World Wide Web: http://www.businessmotivator.com/pressroom_articles/introduction_to_shameles s_self_promo.htm

23. Wikipedia. (2009) Professional Certification. Retrieved July 26, 2009 from the World Wide Web: http://en.wikipedia.org/wiki/Professional_certification

24. Marmolejo, Nancy. (2008) "Facebook Finesse," an interview with Mari Smith audio recording.

25. Starak, Yaro. (2008, February 9) "How To Write Great Blog Content – The Pillar Article." Retrieved July 26, 2009 from the World Wide Web: http://www.entrepreneurs-journey.com/845/pillar-article

About the Author

Nina Price is a Licensed Acupuncturist, speaker, teacher, radio personality, business and wellness coach. She has an MBA from the University of Michigan and has spent 20 years working for well-known high tech firms in the Silicon Valley as a software engineer and marketing manager.

In *5 Strategies for Staying Employed in Today's Economy*, Nina offers her wisdom based on her years of experience in the corporate world and what she's learned since she stepped off the corporate treadmill in 2001.

She's created a simple, step-by-step set of strategies for you to create the life you want. Because she's spent 20 years working in corporations, she knows the issues and challenges you face. She's been where you are and has learned many valuable lessons, which she shares with you in this book.

Nina has also coached hundreds of corporate professionals who are facing the same issues you are and shares some of their learning here, too.

If you're ready to have the life and career you want, rather than the one you have, read this book and find out what you can do to create what you're wishing for. You'll be incredibly pleased with the results.

How to Work with Me

It's about pushing the reset button and taking action!
Take the leap from thinking about taking care of yourself and your career to actually doing it.

Private Coaching or Healthcare

We'll address your health and your career concerns, create a blueprint for what you really want and get you on the path to achieving your dreams. Acupuncture treatments can be a part of the mix but need to be done in person. Coaching is primarily by phone.

Group Coaching or Mastermind Sessions

Allow you to:

Focus on at least one of the 5 Strategies

Pick one of the 5 strategies and delve deep into what you really want to accomplish, then make it happen!

Push the Reset Button

What used to work for you is no longer working. Here's an opportunity to explore new options for the aspects of your life that need them. Take action to create what you really want: the best of health, a satisfying profession, and a life too.

Design the Next Chapter of Your Life

You see a new chapter of your life approaching and want to be prepared to enjoy it. Whether it's a big birthday, an empty nest, a new venture, or other new era, here's your opportunity to develop the ground rules, the boundary conditions, or the lack thereof. Mostly it's about creating what you really want.

Implement Professional Competitiveness

Work through all 5 strategies as they relate to you and your life, with the support of other fellow travelers who are doing the same.

Workshops or Events

Check my website for information about SHARPEN YOUR COMPETITIVE EDGE and other upcoming workshops or events:

- http://www.ninaprice.com or
- http://www.sharpenyourcompetitiveedge.info

Take the first step: email me and tell me what you want to accomplish.
nina@ninaprice.com